FIX THE SYSTEM, NOT THE WOMEN

LAURA BATES

**SIMON &
SCHUSTER**

London · New York · Sydney · Toronto · New Delhi

First published in Great Britain by Simon & Schuster UK Ltd, 2022

1 3 5 7 9 10 8 6 4 2

Simon & Schuster UK Ltd
1st Floor
222 Gray's Inn Road
London WC1X 8HB

www.simonandschuster.co.uk
www.simonandschuster.com.au
www.simonandschuster.co.in

Simon & Schuster Australia, Sydney
Simon & Schuster India, New Delhi

A CIP catalogue record for this book is available from the British Library

Hardback ISBN: 978-1-3985-1433-1
eBook ISBN: 978-1-3985-1434-8

Typeset in Perpetua by M Rules
Printed in the UK by CPI Group (UK) Ltd, Croydon, CR0 4YY

MIX
Paper from
responsible sources
FSC® C171272

Praise for *Men Who Hate Women*

'Brilliantly fierce and eye-opening' *Guardian*

'Profoundly important . . . a book everyone should read' *Observer*

'Excellent . . . has the power to spark social change' *Sunday Times*

'Laura Bates is showing us the path to both intimate and global survival' Gloria Steinem

'Brilliant . . . a brave new book shows why we should all be afraid' *Independent*

Praise for *Everyday Sexism*

'Thrilling, intelligent, accessible, uplifting and empowering. Read the book' Lucy Mangan, *Stylist*

'Shocking, powerful, passionate' *Sunday Times*

'Will make most women feel oddly saner' Caitlin Moran

*For my wonderful mum, for being there
every single step of the way.*

CONTENTS

FIX THE SYSTEM, NOT THE WOMEN

THE LIST

'I have so many stories. Too many to list . . . There's
too many stories to even remember, let alone tell.'

Everyday Sexism Project entry[*]

My list, like most, starts before I'm even conscious of it. It starts
with the ugly, heavy piece of gold jewellery my mum finds on the
passenger seat of the car as she and my dad leave my grandparents'
house after visiting to introduce them to my new baby brother.
The gift is there because, after two daughters, she's finally had a
son. I am five years old and have no idea I've already been weighed,
valued and found wanting.

At primary school, I'm baffled by 'jokes' about women with
small feet who can fit closer to the kitchen sink, kids who think
'make me a sandwich' is an effective insult, and the total playground segregation between footballing boys and skipping girls.

---

[*] Unless stated otherwise, all the stories quoted in this book are drawn from the
Everyday Sexism Project.

Before the age of eight, I'm pressured into 'selecting' which boy I will marry (I panic and offer my cousin's name). Before the age of nine, my best friend runs straight into a wall and loses half her front tooth, so desperate is she to get away from the pursuing boys in a game of kiss chase. On school coach trips, kids pass around papers with numbers corresponding to sexual acts and the names of boys in our year group. You have to pick two numbers and withstand the screams of mirth and mockery about what you've 'done' with whom. When my dad later finds the paper crumpled in my school bag, I dissolve in horror and hot shame. I want to say that I don't know what it is and I didn't want to do it, but I can't.

When I am thirteen, I come out of the changing rooms for a swimming lesson and listen to the boys rating the girls' bodies out of ten. I feel furious, terrified, ashamed and humiliated. None of the girls say a word. I learn that, among my peer group, a girl's value is measured by how many boys find her attractive and want to have sex with her. I hear boys in my class describing girls as 'slags' and 'thunder thighs'. Male peers mock me for my indignation when they pass around a 'magic' pen with a picture of a woman that can be tipped upside down to slowly remove her clothes. The games at the back of the bus now involve spin the bottle and 'chicken' – where a boy runs his hand up the inside of your leg towards your crotch until you are 'cowardly' enough to stop him.

As I begin to move through the world, the lessons accumulate. Not just the lessons I learn at school, but outside, too. By the age of fourteen, I have been followed, whistled at, shouted at, catcalled and propositioned more times than I can count. I have learned to flinch when a man I don't know comes towards me in the street. I have learned to cross the street if I see a group of men together on the pavement. I never feel completely safe in a public space, but I am not really conscious of this and I cannot put my finger on the exact moment it began. It is just my reality.

I read endless magazine features about flaws I didn't even realise I had and all the many things I should be doing to fix them. I skim a copy of a women's weekly that carries a 'circle of shame' on the front cover, highlighting the publication's disgust at a female celebrity's cellulite or stomach rolls. In my early teens, I start secretly buying SlimFast milkshakes and hiding them in my school desk. I suck in my stomach every moment of every day. My body shape is average, but my emotional relationship with it becomes fraught and torturous. No matter what else is happening in my life – exams, friendships, music lessons, school plays – I am rarely not worrying about whether I look fat. Locked in my bedroom at night, I faithfully follow a 'holiday body bootcamp' exercise regime ripped out of a magazine, repeating it over and over again. Before going on holiday, I stop eating almost altogether. I ration myself to a handful of cereal for breakfast and one for lunch. When we go out for a meal on the first night away, my body is so unused to rich food that I spend the rest of the night vomiting in the bathroom, trying to keep quiet so my family won't notice what is happening.

At school, we have one session just for the girls where a policeman tells the girls to shout 'fire' instead of 'rape' if they are attacked. People are more likely to respond, apparently. I think the boys are playing football at the time. No lesson at school ever covers anything related to sexual consent or healthy relationships, let alone rape, coercion or abuse. So, when a boy does something to me that I don't want to happen, I don't know how to say no, how to stop him, how to do anything but freeze. I sit on the toilet afterwards and look at the blood and I never, ever tell anybody what happened.

In my mid-teens, when I wear a close-fitting top with a caption on the front, a male teacher stops me in the corridor, holds my shoulders and slowly, leerily reads each word aloud. When I confide to another teacher that we need the costume department to purchase slips because the white dresses we've been provided to wear in a theatre production are see-through, he grins and tells me (in front of my mostly male classmates), 'But we like to see your underwear.' Another male teacher sits on the edge of a girl's desk in an English class, pouts and asks her, 'Do you think I'm sexy?'

At fifteen, I receive inappropriate emails from a senior male colleague at my part-time holiday job; I am called into a manager's office to be reprimanded for causing this, having worn a short skirt. Around this time, men in the street start telling me to smile or cheer up because it 'might never happen'. It doesn't seem to occur to them that maybe I'm no longer smiling in public spaces because it already has.

At the end of each year, there is a Christmas party in our school houses during which girls compete at licking cream off upright bananas while long lists of gossip about various dalliances and activities with different boys are read out with great hilarity. When I'm in the sixth form, a new teacher, recently arrived, asks me if it has occurred to me that the entire occasion reduces girls entirely to their sexual experiences, positioning them only in terms of their relationship to their male peers. I look at her blankly. It has not occurred to me that any other approach is possible. When we arrive at the school Christmas dinner, the boys already assembled start barking uproariously and singing 'Who Let the Dogs Out' at the top of their voices.

At university, I am lined up and ranked by appearance at a social; the boys ask if they can pick which of the girls they want to escort in to dinner based on the value of the bottle of wine they have brought with them. There is a professor at my college who wears a black armband every year to mourn the day women were admitted to the college. My boyfriend goes to the end-of-year football dinner and comes back with a trophy: the 'under the thumb' award for the player who is considered too 'whipped' by his girlfriend.

By the time I leave university, aged twenty, I have been sexually assaulted, pressured to perform topless in a theatre production (I stand my ground, but the experience leaves me in tears) and cornered in the street by two men shouting, 'We're going to part those legs and fuck that cunt.'

A member of my family expresses dismay that my brother has chosen to study languages at university, apparently an inappropriate and unimpressive subject. When I protest that I studied English, the relative laughs. 'It doesn't matter what you studied. You're a girl.'

Arriving at auditions in a fledgling acting career, I am, on one occasion, told to take my top off; on another, I am directed into a darkened room with another girl and asked to make louder and louder orgasm noises until the casting director is satisfied. I audition for an advert in which a man sits on a porch drinking beer while a girl suggestively pops out from under the blanket draped across his lap, suggesting she has been giving him oral sex. At another audition, I'm paired with a young actor for a scene in which a group of men are so desperate to escape their nagging, diet-obsessed wives at a fancy spa that they use their dinner cutlery to tunnel to freedom (and, of course, a cool beer). When I say that the script is kind of sexist, my audition partner tetchily tells me that it's actually very true to life: it reflects the dynamic of every couple he knows.

I move to London where I am followed home by a man refusing to take no for an answer; I find my breasts loudly rated and comments made about my vagina by strangers in the street; I sit terrified in a Tube carriage as a mob of boys on the platform run after my train, banging on the window as it pulls away and shouting at me. Two men sit near me and publicly masturbate under their coats, one in a shopping centre and another on a bus, their eyes drilling into mine as though daring me to do anything about it. I am sexually assaulted again, this time on a public bus. I say what is happening out loud, but nobody does anything to help me.

I have my body parts appraised in the street too many times to list. Once, a man turns to his friend as I pass them on a darkened street and says, 'I'd hold a knife to that.' Another day, as I walk down a quiet road, a group of men in a van drive past. Slowing down and opening the sliding door, they mime dragging me in. I run away, not knowing whether or not they are 'joking'. I'm left shaking, but also feeling ashamed at my reaction because, after all, 'nothing really happened'.

All these things are connected. They all happen because I am a girl. Later, because I am a woman. And most of them seem completely normal to me. It will be more than twenty years after those first early experiences that I will start the Everyday Sexism Project and begin to join the dots.

If this list sounds shocking, it isn't. It is ordinary.

This is an incomplete list. Some of it I've talked about before; some I haven't. That's okay. I'm not ready to share it all. And I don't have to be. You don't have to share yours either, if you don't want to. But it can help to allow yourself to see it.

Because, if you are a woman, you are likely to have a list like this, too. It might look very different to mine. It may well be intermingled with experiences of racism, homophobia, ageism, classism, ableism, transphobia, Islamophobia, anti-Semitism or other forms of prejudice. You may be very aware of it or you may never have thought about it before. This doesn't mean it isn't real or that it hasn't affected you. Just thinking about it might come as a shock. This might sound strange, given that you have lived it, but we are taught to suppress, to accept, to swallow, to absorb and to carry so much that it can take time and sometimes painful effort to remember.

At first, there are the obvious incidents, the ones that spring quickly to mind. The ones that stand out. But, the more you think about it, the more you are likely to recall and to question. The smaller things. The ones that really stung, but you convinced yourself you were being over-sensitive about. The ones other people told you not to make a fuss over, not to take the wrong way. The ones other people told you not to make a fuss about, not to take the wrong way. The tiny ones. The ones you know were not intended with malice. The ones you didn't trust yourself to judge. Did I imagine it? Am I making a fuss about nothing? Surely that didn't really happen? There will be items on your list that you have buried for years. Things you doubt. It can be painful to allow them to resurface. You will hear other people's voices, dismissing, minimising, even as you start to remember. Was it my fault? Did I do something to deserve it? Was I leading him on?

You will ask yourself these questions because they have been asked of you your whole life. Were you asking for it? Are you exaggerating? Are you sure? Do you really want to make a fuss about this?

When you experience something your whole life, it can be hard to allow yourself to see it, let alone to recognise it as something out of the ordinary. Something wrong. It's even harder when you've been trained, nudged or, in some cases, forced to dismiss these incidents, instead of acknowledging, discussing or reporting them, and when other people have reacted to them as though they are normal. Or funny. Or your fault. Shame and silencing can be very difficult to unpick.

In early 2012, by coincidence, I experienced a number of such incidents in just one week. I was shouted at in the street. I was followed by a man sexually harassing me. Another man touched me inappropriately on the bus. On each occasion, I responded as I had been conditioned to: I tried to ignore it. I felt the prickly heat of shame and anger crawling up my neck; I felt my heart rate speed up with the familiar fear; I looked straight ahead, got off the bus and walked home. I didn't tell anyone. I never dreamed of reporting anything. But, for the first time ever, I joined the dots. I recognised that these incidents were connected. I realised that, if they hadn't occurred so close together, I might never have thought twice about any one of them. I realised they were common.

This prompted me to think about my list and about how many similar experiences I'd had over the years – at university, in part-time jobs, at school, in public spaces. For the first time ever, I questioned the ways in which my life had been shaped by fear, abuse, harassment, discrimination – all purely based on my sex. And I wondered if I was the only one. So I started asking other women about their lists. A friend had been harassed moments before I asked her the question. Another said that she missed out on business deals on a weekly basis because her male colleagues entertained clients at strip clubs without inviting her. A third said that her ticket at a work function was repeatedly checked by a security guard who asked her what she was doing there and used the opportunity to leer at her, though her white colleagues had been admitted without incident. The racism she had experienced was inextricably intertwined with the gendered elements of her list.

When I asked women about their lists, they were usually sur-
prised. Nobody had ever asked before. Very often they said, 'I've
never told anyone.' When I asked why, the response was almost
universal: 'Because it's normal.'

I didn't think it should be normal any more. And I didn't think
we should be keeping quiet about it, even if we'd been taught
to do so our whole lives. So, a month or two later, I started the
Everyday Sexism Project – a very simple website where people
could share their stories. Stories of any kind of gender inequality. Sexist jokes. Street harassment. Workplace discrimination.
Sexual assault. I hoped that maybe fifty people would share their
stories. Instead, at the time of writing, over 200,000 posts have
flooded in, from all over the world.

At first, the stories all seemed so different. The woman whose
boss sexually harassed her so appallingly that she left her position
without another job to go to. The sex worker who met ridicule
when she attempted to report her rape to the police. The black
woman whose preparations to give the keynote presentation at a
conference were repeatedly interrupted by other attendees asking
her to bring them refreshments or show them to the bathroom,
assuming that she was a member of catering staff. The disabled
woman who was told to do a pole dance around her walking stick
in a public space. The child who didn't fully understand the men
shouting at her in her uniform on her way to school because what
they said was so sexually explicit. The young woman who tried
to ignore two men catcalling her from their car, only to find they
screeched to a halt and tried to drag her in. The junior doctor
assaulted from behind by a senior male colleague when she asked
for his help interpreting an X-ray. The twelve- and sixteen-year-
old sisters trying to picnic in a public park when a man came and
exposed himself to them. The young Muslim woman who was

accused of besmirching family 'honour' when she dared to speak out against abuse. The girls at a private Catholic school who were forced to sit through a presentation about 'wicked' women murdering babies when choosing to have abortions. The student told by her university professor, 'You look prettier when you shut up.'

As the stories poured in, it became clear that there were enormous overlaps between the different forms of oppression seen in so many of the testimonies. (The term 'intersectionality', which describes this overlap and interaction, was coined by lawyer, scholar and advocate Professor Kimberlé Crenshaw.) Institutional racism. People with disabilities systemically failed. Heteronormative societal foundations. Class barriers. Fatphobia. Prejudice on the grounds of religion, gender identity, mental health, immigration status. Or, as the late author, professor and activist bell hooks described it, the 'white supremacist, capitalist patriarchy' – a term she uses to describe 'the interlocking systems of domination that define our reality . . . a shortcut way of saying all of these things actually are functioning simultaneously at all times in our lives'.

The black woman who declined a man's unwanted sexual advances only to have him call her the 'n word' and order her to 'get out of his country'. The trans woman who found that catcalling and street harassment escalated to physical abuse the moment the perpetrators realised she was transgender. The Filipino woman who was told by a man, 'You're cute, but I'm just not into chinky girls.' The school dress codes that clamp down unfairly and disproportionately on everything from colourful hijabs to black girls' hairstyles. The Muslim women bombarded with misogynistic and Islamophobic abuse on dating apps from men telling them things like, 'I want to unravel your burka and defuse you.' The disabled women who described being aggressively accosted by men demanding medical details and asking inappropriate questions about their sex lives. One was told she should be grateful for sexual harassment because 'at least an able-bodied man was interested in you'. The lesbians weary of the fact that, 'if you tell an obnoxious guy you like girls, they don't take it as a rejection, they take it as a chance for a threesome' and say things like, 'It's okay, baby, I can just watch.' Indeed, one woman recalled telling a man at a party that she was a lesbian, to which he responded by taking out his penis and saying, 'Just hold it.' When she recounted this to a friend, they didn't believe her.

These stories reveal how intertwined and cumulative experiences of prejudice are.

> I choose to wear loose dresses and a scarf on my head and am pretty much completely covered except for my hands and face. I choose this way of dressing for myself (though most of my friends are not Muslim, so they don't cover) because I feel that it expresses my values and who I am and I love to be able to proudly say, 'Yes, this is my religion!' A little while ago, I was walking down the street to uni and a big guy stepped in front of me. I was a bit confused and couldn't hear what he was saying, so I took out my headphones ... I heard him asking me, 'Do you speak English?' I answered 'yes', thinking that maybe he needed help or directions or was asking for money, but, the second the word came out of my mouth, he got in my face and started shouting at me. 'You speak English and you are dressed that way?! What do you think you are doing?! I'll tell you: you're a stupid cunt, that's what you are. Just a stupid bitch!'

I read all the stories as they came in, poring over them late at night, approving them for publication myself after a surge of abusive messages, rape and death threats had forced me to switch to a pre-moderated system for project entries. It struck me that there was a connection between the stories of sexism, harassment and assault and the attitudes of the men threatening to shut the project down by raping me into submission. They didn't even see the irony. 'Let me demonstrate to you that sexism doesn't exist with my violent sexist abuse.' The misogyny of the men telling me they hoped I died or those theorising about how spectacularly ugly I must be in order to run such a project or those threatening to find me and force pieces of furniture and weaponry into my body. They were part of it. They were proof of exactly the kind of widespread, normalised misogyny I was trying to expose. And you couldn't separate one from the other.

Both could only arise from a society in which the sexual objectification, harassment and oppression of women were commonplace and in which the superiority, privilege and entitlement of usually white, heterosexual, non-disabled men went unchallenged. We'd all been thinking of these stories as individual problems – our own personal, coincidental lists. But they weren't. They were connected. And that meant that the problem wasn't with us; it was with the system.

Since I started the project a decade ago, I have heard so many other women's lists. Hastily sketched out on the bus. Laughed at in pub toilets. Cried over in private. Written in project entries thousands of words long. Whispered at the end of book events by teenage girls who waited for everyone else to disappear before finding the courage to come forward, to share this load, this list longer than anyone should ever have to carry, let alone a girl who is just fourteen years old. Everybody's list is different.

But, no matter what the background or life experience of the woman, I've noticed all the lists have a lot in common. In the delivery, the doubt, the almost apologies. In the 'I know how lucky I am' and the 'it could have been worse'. In the sudden memory of other incidents, half-forgotten or forcibly buried, and the extent to which they want me to confirm it; yearning for the absolute proof of somebody else's authority to give them permission to mourn, to grieve, to get angry. Because, when it comes to our lists, we have been trained, systematically, not to trust ourselves. We have also been trained not to think about these lists at all. Not to make them. Not to count them. Not to connect the dots. Trained to view them as isolated incidents. Or not to believe they were experiences of discrimination or abuse at all.

Perhaps the first, simplest, smallest, most urgent act of resistance each of us can take is to make our lists. Sit. Think. Write. Let yourself feel it. Allow yourself the rage of realising that there are more and more and more moments you'd forgotten – lost or stolen from you by the indifference of passers-by or the dismissal of those you loved and trusted. Let yourself reclaim them. Let yourself see this as a whole, each experience part of a bigger story. Not 'just a misunderstanding'. Not 'just a compliment'. Not 'overreacting'. Not 'taking it the wrong way'. Not 'boys being boys'. But sexual harassment. Not 'groping' or 'banter'. But sexual assault. Not 'sex where you didn't really consent'. But rape. You don't have to use those labels if you don't want to, but you are the one who gets to decide.

Let yourself have your list. That is your story. What you do with it is up to you. But it is nobody else's to take away from you, to deny, dismiss, belittle or obliterate with well-meaning platitudes or sexist, outdated excuses. It is yours and yours alone. It is real.

And it matters. Because, once we start seeing these lists as our history, our heritage, part of who we are, we can also see the enormous and extensive impact they have. We start to see how they've crept into our story of ourselves, their impact extending far, far beyond the initial incidents.

> I am a 49-year-old woman and have so many stories, I don't even know where to begin. I don't have any of the horrific tales of assault that so many of the women on here have been brave enough to share – just a lifetime of male harassment. I want to start by saying sorry to younger women. I'm sorry I bore all this so silently, that I didn't report most of it or scream out loud about what was happening to me. I'm sorry I stayed so quiet, it meant that the world was not made better for you. Please understand all this behaviour was normalised and happening to all of my friends, too. We barely even talked about it . . . This is not normal. None of it is normal. I want better for my daughter – and all of you.

It is extraordinary, really, that we live in a society that has managed to pull off the most incredible feat of silencing. A society in which almost all women have these long, trailing lists of stories, yet where so many of us still feel utterly alone in them. Where we are so effectively silenced, from such a young age, that we never have the realisation that we are not alone. And that is such a powerful way of oppressing us. Because, as long as you think you are the only one, it is so easy to think that you might be wrong, might be imagining it, might be to blame, might be being over-sensitive. That maybe you've been doing something wrong, been asking for it, been unlucky, been in the wrong place at the wrong time. In short, it makes it much more difficult to see your experiences as part of a systemic problem. And, if you can't see the system, you can't fight it.

As time went by, as the number of stories gradually ticked over from 100 to 1,000 and then 10,000, I started to see little sparks. Tendrils creeping out from one apparently unique story and connecting it to another. Links emerging between quite dramatically different incidents. The connections stretched between stories like colourful wires, crisscrossing the project database, linking the experiences of these 200,000 women over and over again until I started to see it not as a collection of individual entries at all, but as a pattern. A map with contours and highways and detours, with tributaries that lead to rivers that cause floods.

These things, which we are, at worst, encouraged to dismiss altogether or, at best, primed to think of as 'separate' issues, are really part of a spectrum. There is a continuum of gender inequality, with wolf whistles, catcalls, sexist jokes, gendered language and sweeping stereotypes occupying one end, while rape, domestic abuse, forced marriage, female genital mutilation and so-called 'honour' killings sit at the other, with maternity discrimination, workplace sexual harassment, the gender pay gap and so much more lying somewhere in between. This doesn't mean we are 'ranking' or comparing these different issues, but simply recognising the connections and complex context that links them all. We have to be allowed to talk about the 'minor' things as though they matter – because they do. Because the low-level attitudes and behaviours we cement with the thousands of 'little', 'unimportant' things we don't talk about are the foundation of more serious abuses.

And, just as we fail to join the dots in our own lives, we also fail to see the connections in our society. The more you think about it, the more absurd it is that people believe we can usefully talk about something like sexual violence without discussing the criminal justice system; that a discussion about domestic abuse can be complete without recognising that the roots of power and control begin in childhood and are also plainly on display in the dynamics of our political system; that anyone thinks it is possible to have a conversation about rape that isn't simultaneously about education and what is happening in schools.

You can see how looking at individual cases, divorced from the context of their backdrop, homogenises them – as though one woman who has been raped represents all women who have been raped or one maternity discrimination case is identical to another – when, in reality, the experience and needs of each woman may be drastically different based on her own complex set of circumstances and the impact of various systems on her life. The marital rape of a woman trapped in an abusive relationship; the 'corrective' rape of a lesbian refugee trying desperately to convince disbelieving authorities to give her leave to remain; the rape of a child in a school, where she is subsequently slut-shamed by her peers; the rape of a sex worker who is told she implicitly consented by virtue of her means of making money; the rape of a man who never receives support because he is made to feel that speaking out about it would be emasculating; the rape of a fifteen-year-old girl in care who is invisible to authorities as they simply think she has 'made a lifestyle choice'. Yes, these are all rapes. But it is so much more complicated than that. If we aren't allowed to make connections, to recognise the different systems and inequalities at play, to show how oppression in one sphere of life impacts the treatment of women in another, then how can we possibly begin to move forward?

But people do not seem to want to see these links. If I am invited to speak on the radio about the challenges faced by women in politics, I will be chastised for straying off the topic when I try to bring the issue of sexism in the media into the discussion. An editor advised me to stay focused on the issue at hand when a draft of a proposed article about sexual assault included an appraisal of the education system's failings to tackle gender stereotyping. I have been invited to take part in radio discussions about feminist history that didn't include the voice of any women of colour and fixated exclusively on the experiences of middle-class white women.

The moments of connection and clarity when we allow ourselves to speak freely about these experiences can be enormously, overwhelmingly cathartic. The elderly woman who sent me a typewritten letter expressing her relief at reading other women's experiences and realising at last, after decades of painful shame, that her sexual assault had not, in fact, been her own fault. The abuse survivor who shook and cried as she stood in a book-signing queue and told me her story. The tears I have quietly held back as some women have told me stories that are precisely identical to my own. And, even now, the moment of sheer shock when you look around you and realise that the thing you have been made to feel was your own personal misfortune is actually a shared experience of structural oppression.

The moment you compare notes with other women on the long, long list of ways you work, every single day, to keep yourself safe. The keys between your knuckles, the texts when you're safely home, the hand over your glass in the bar. That furious recognition that we are all doing the same things. The absurdity of talking to men about this list and realising they have absolutely no idea what we are talking about . . .

Or the casual conversation about how you and your female friends deal with unwanted 'dick pics'. Some delete, block and move on; some keep them in a folder to send back to future offenders (hey, he obviously loves pictures of dicks, right?); some click on their profiles and forward the messages on to their mothers to make a point. If you ask a woman how many of these images she has received in the past year, she will probably run out of fingers to count on. But, when you turn to a man and ask him how many unsolicited vulvas he has seen recently, he is likely to look at you like you're mad. It's just another example of the obstacle course of sexism, harassment and sexual abuse we navigate daily. But it has become such familiar terrain under our feet – and we have become so expert at dodging, jumping and climbing – that we don't even realise we are navigating it.

How did we get here? How did we reach a point that we can be so shaped by these experiences and yet so blinkered to them? Why does it so often take another woman speaking out for us to recognise our own legitimacy for the first time?

The truth is that it isn't about us at all. It is about the world around us and the way it is shaped. I have identified five ecosystems in which institutional change is necessary, starting with identifying and acknowledging the problem and then tackling it at a systemic level. They are: education; policing; criminal justice; politics; and media – and each of them is suffused with institutional inequality. The sexism that runs through these institutions is normalised and exacerbated by the gender inequality in our culture. Our day-to-day attitudes and behaviours towards women prepare us not to notice the extent of the problem or how deeply embedded it is in the very bones of our society. The only meaningful way to move forward is to embrace root-and-branch reform across these institutions – the kind of bold reboot that nobody will even entertain as long as we keep thinking the current system is normal, 'this is just the way things are', 'nothing is wrong'. Nothing will truly change until we acknowledge that the problem is with the system, not the women.

IT BEGINS

Almost from birth, we are trained and socialised in a world in which the inevitability of male aggression and dominance and the importance of pretty, pliant female submission is completely normalised.

These messages come from all sides.

The summer camp offering a 'finishing school' for girls aged between three and ten to learn 'social etiquette' and a 'future heroes mini business school' for boys to learn 'practical life skills'.

The leading retailer offering a girls' school shoe called 'Dolly Babe' and a boys' equivalent called 'Leader'.

The birthday cards for one-year-olds in which boys are described as sporty 'all-stars' while girls are 'cute' and 'sweet'.

The 'free games' section on popular electronic devices that offers 'aim and shoot' in 'games for boys', but 'ice princess mermaid salon' for girls. Or, on another platform, 'bike race' for boys and 'dress-up and make-up' for girls.

The gendered 'brave knight' and 'perfect princess' lunch boxes.

The graduation cards in the same store that read: 'You're going to change the world' in the boys' section; 'It's rare to find a young woman who knows who she is' in the girls' section.

The in-flight magazine offering pilot T-shirts to be purchased for boys, but cabin-crew dresses for girls.

Even the magnetic fridge words designed to help children learn to read are unnecessarily and perniciously gendered: the blue 'boys talk' version containing words like 'mud', 'dirt', 'frogs', 'helicopter', 'wizard', 'car', 'dragon', 'dinosaur', while the 'girls talk' version includes 'clothes', 'hairband', 'heart', 'love', 'sparkle', 'perfume', 'fluff', 'princess' and 'cooking'.

How early does it start? Well, as soon as babies begin drooling, gendered bibs are offered. 'Boy genius' reads one; 'Ready for my #selfie' proclaims the pink alternative. Before these infants have even learned to walk, a major clothing retailer encourages parents to buy girls 'a dress for photo-ops and first twirls' and boys a pair of 'ready-to-crawl' trousers to 'protect little knees'. As the toddlers get a little bigger, a mainstream supermarket advertises its girls' trousers: 'Find the perfect gift for a little princess . . . oh-so-pretty pastels . . . will have her looking cute as a button.' The boys' range says: 'Your active little man needs clothes that will move with him. Our baby boys' trousers are all comfy styles that will mean he can be as busy as he likes.' When the children get to that exciting 'first bike' stage, a well-known cycling store offers a 'pink hearts bike helmet . . . for lovely little girls who really enjoy playing on their bikes and looking really pretty', whereas a 'blue flames' bike helmet is on sale for 'boys [who are] ready for action . . . sporty and cool'.

Look at these slogans on kids' T-shirts, vests and pyjamas from the same stores in the past few years alone:

REAL SLOGANS ON BOYS' T-SHIRTS	REAL SLOGANS ON GIRLS' T-SHIRTS
The Little Scholar	The Social Butterfly
Mummy's Little Soldier	Mummy's Little Cupcake
Stormtrooper	Kindness Counts
Be Your Own Superhero	Daddy is My Superhero
Little Genius	Princess in Training
Little Man Big Ideas	Little Girl Big Smiles
King of the Castle	Pretty Little Me
Hero	Beautiful
Think Outside the Box	I Feel Fabulous
I'm Super!	I Hate My Thighs
Lock Up Your Daughters	Does this Diaper Make My Butt Look Big?
Run, Jump, Flip, Repeat	Try, Fail, Fix Ponytail, Try Again
Future Man of Steel	I Only Date Heroes

It's not just girls who are affected by this. The slogans and messaging aimed at boys repeatedly suggest that they are less worthy of love, cuddles and kisses, that they should be independent, powerful and strong, and that it is only acceptable for girls to show vulnerability and emotion or to reach out for help. Later on, all this will reach its logical, devastating conclusion in the fact that suicide is the leading cause of death for men under fifty.

And early notions of controlling, male-dominated sexual relationships are already being normalised. Take the boys' T-shirts that read 'Sorry Ladies I Only Date Models' and 'Chicks All Over Me', for example, compared to girls' clothing with slogans like 'I'm Not Allowed to Date Ever'.

This messaging has real consequences in setting the foundations for gendered power dynamics in relationships and even sexual violence. 'Boys will be boys' isn't just an underlying message in our society; we're literally printing it on children's sweatshirts and selling it in supermarkets for £4.

But it isn't only the norms and dynamics of sexual violence that can be linked to these early messages. They affect our whole lives. Studies have repeatedly shown that, by the age of six, girls already perceive women to be less 'brilliant' and smart than men and that they have already begun to apply these stereotypes to themselves. This continues into adulthood, with men repeatedly being shown to estimate their own intelligence more highly than women do.

The stories from teenage girls who are distressed at seeing unrealistic, airbrushed models so ubiquitously are linked to the testimonies of older women whose lives have been consumed for decades by eating disorders, yo-yo dieting and low self-esteem. As one commented: 'It has taken a long time before I realised that I wasn't going to look like the girls in the movies, games and cartoons. It took even longer to realise that it was okay.'

The stories from little boys who are bullied or punished for picking up a toy doll are connected to the tales from men who are ridiculed and dismissed when they ask for extended parental leave from work. And those, in turn, are connected to the experiences of women who lose their jobs because they become pregnant and are told, 'You won't have time to focus on your clients any more.'

The fact that sexism starts from an incredibly young age completely normalises it. When we've been immersed in these slogans and messages our whole lives, it is difficult for us to recognise them as problematic or biased.

Clinical psychologist Dr Sophie Mort tells me:

> These entrenched gender roles shape our behaviour from a young age, preventing many girls from believing they, too, can be leaders, that they, too, can be confident, and that they, too, have more to themselves than being pretty or kind (not that there's anything wrong with being pretty or kind), meaning they often end up shrinking themselves to fit the roles they have been given, affecting not only their esteem and confidence, but also the choices they will make as they choose school, university [or] training subjects and career roles.

Of course, one of the reasons we so readily internalise and accept these norms is that they don't just come in external messages from the media, consumer products, shops and the world around us. They also, painfully, come from the people we trust the most. From our own families and communities. Worse still, the normalisation of inequality is even reinforced at school.

Schools

As a child, I would regularly get catcalled and have obscene gestures directed towards me from men many years older than me, often twice my age or more. I was told by my family and by teachers, both in primary and secondary school, that they probably just really liked me. I was also told from about the age of twelve, that

I should wear baggier clothing as I was overdeveloped for my age and this was probably confusing them.

On average in the UK, one rape per school day is reported to the police as having occurred on school premises. Almost a third of teenage girls say they've been sexually assaulted at school. Almost 80 per cent of girls say sexual assault happens 'sometimes' or 'a lot' between people their age at secondary schools and colleges. Ninety per cent say that being sent unsolicited 'dick pics' happens to them or their peers 'sometimes' or 'a lot', while 92 per cent describe recurrent sexist name-calling. Three-quarters of girls report that pressure to provide sexual images of themselves happens 'sometimes' or 'a lot' and over 70 per cent say that images they sent were shared more widely. Almost 60 per cent report being photographed or videoed without consent.

Ofsted inspectors carrying out an inquiry into sexual harassment in schools in 2021 were told by pupils that sexual harassment had become completely normal – such a routine part of girls' daily lives that they don't see any point in challenging or reporting it. This is very much confirmed by tens of thousands of Everyday Sexism Project entries.

While some teachers and individual schools put huge effort into tackling these issues with sensitivity and leadership, it is still devastatingly common for girls to experience sexual violence at school. And, like other forms of schooling, these are very formative experiences. Schools, and later universities, become yet another link in the long chain of institutions that replicate, exacerbate and enforce inequality.

How can any of us be expected to grow up understanding that abuse is wrong, that we have the right to control our own bodies and that we shouldn't just 'put up' with sexual harassment when these experiences are rife and treated as 'the way things are' in the very place we go to learn? This is a very effective form of 'education'. Learning that we are less. Learning that we have to accept it. Learning that nobody will take us seriously or do anything, even if we object.

Learning that we will be blamed. That it is all our own fault. That the problem is not with the system, but with us.

I've met girls who've been called into their headteacher's office to be reprimanded for trying to start a feminist society because it might be 'too divisive' and upset the boys. I've met girls who have been suspended after nude photographs of them have been circulated without their consent, while the boys sharing the photographs have gone unpunished. I've met black girls who have been accused of being 'too sexy' simply for wearing the same school uniform as their white peers, their bodies policed in different ways by their school. I've also seen how black girls who try to fight back or speak up after being sexually harassed are more frequently dismissed as 'making trouble' and are more likely to be punished or excluded from school than their peers.

> I cannot pick a fight with every other builder on a street corner who tells me – a fourteen-year-old – that I have nice tits. I cannot argue with every classmate who tells me 'rape is just rough sex' and that 'it feels good after a while'. I, a schoolgirl, am utterly powerless against the people who would objectify me. I have this raging, hot anger inside me.

In 2021, when boys were caught taking photographs up the skirts of girls on a transparent glass staircase at a Catholic school in Liverpool, the school reportedly responded by telling girls to start wearing shorts under their school skirts. Former pupils told the media that they had complained about the issue with the staircase for years. One ex-pupil commented to the *Liverpool Echo*: 'Within school, you're meant to be taught lessons for the future and this will just allow these boys to think this behaviour is acceptable. Girls within this school or any school shouldn't have to deal with sexual harassment on a daily basis.' Female pupils from the same school reported that they had been sent home for wearing pencil skirts 'because they were "inappropriate"'.

This was not an isolated incident. Headline after headline reports with alarming frequency how girls are being sent home from school for 'showing thigh', 'inappropriately' revealing their (gasp) shoulders, and even having visible bra straps. If the *Handmaid's Tale* vibes here weren't obvious enough, one US school actually edited the yearbook photos of eighty girls to remove pretty much all traces of skin below the collarbone using a Photoshop job so shoddy it looked like a five-year-old had been let loose with the original version of Microsoft Paint. The (completely unremarkable) original photos were 'deemed inappropriate' by the school. Shockingly, not one of the boys' photos was considered in need of any alteration.

This is indoctrination on a mass scale: we are systematically teaching children to blame, shame and sexualise women's bodies. We are stigmatising individual women via a system in which their functional body parts are considered to be explosively dangerous and unacceptable.

In sixth form college, the girls were all told that we had to wear shirts WITH LONG SLEEVES because some of the male teachers were finding it distracting. 1. It was the middle of summer; 2. The boys were allowed to wear whatever they wanted to;

3. None of our male teachers were under forty and all were married, mostly with children; 4. We were sixteen/seventeen years old at the time. Men need to learn to control themselves if SHOULDERS are too sexy for them to cope with in a professional/educational environment.

The idea that boys will inevitably harass, that girls are responsible for 'protecting themselves', and that female bodies are to blame for making boys act badly are all conveyed to young people at an impressionable age by their own educational institutions. Schools echo and reinforce mainstream beauty standards that privilege and normalise thin, white bodies and alienate and shame others. Girls' self-doubt, self-blame and self-consciousness are all amplified. Boys' sense of impunity and their knowledge that the system will work in their favour are given powerful foundations. The likelihood that girls will blame themselves if sexually assaulted is increased. The likelihood that boys will not recognise their behaviour as problematic or even downright illegal when they sexually harass or assault is increased.

Most ironic of all, considering how frantic schools seem to be to prevent girls from being 'sexy', the schools themselves are sexualising girls' bodies before the girls themselves even make that choice. For example, a five-year-old child was forced to change her clothes at *nursery* because her summer dress had spaghetti straps, while a nine-year-old was suspended for wearing 'form-fitting' clothes.

In other words, many schools, instead of providing opportunities to critique and question the gender stereotyping, misogyny and abuse pupils will already be encountering in the wider world, simply reinforce the issues instead. And so schools become another part of the system.

And, while dress codes are a particularly useful microcosm

for how education can be institutionally misogynistic, they are certainly not the only example. Everything from school curricula dominated by white, male authors, composers, philosophers and historical figures to the fact that 40 per cent of UK universities have no specific reporting tools for sexual misconduct ingrains and perpetuates the cycle of sexualised violence and sexist norms, generation after generation. Research into Key Stage 3 texts, for example, found that 75 per cent of pupils aged between eleven and fourteen never read a book or play by a woman, while 84 per cent of texts taught have a male protagonist. In the place where they go to learn, children are taught that this is normal.

Indeed, school teaches us all, from early childhood, that men are the centre of the world and women revolve around them. That men make things happen and women make things look pretty. That men chase careers, achievements, wealth, and that women chase . . . well, men.

Even now, the Everyday Sexism Project is inundated with stories from girls who have been subtly discouraged from pursuing science or engineering, have been told that it's 'understandable' when they struggle with a maths problem because 'it tends to come easier to boys', or have encountered surprise and consternation when they express a desire to study architecture or computer science. Even now, girls are being convinced that the main reason to go to university is to gain their 'M-R-S' degree: in other words, to find a husband.

A girl at a school in the Home Counties told me how, with no warning or preparation, students were ushered into an auditorium to be taught by a visiting male speaker that 'no woman should ever be allowed an abortion, in any circumstances', that 'the majority of women regret abortions' and that 'men should have an equal say over a woman's choice to terminate a pregnancy'. Afterwards, she said, 'A lot of the boys [made] fun of the girls for being angry . . . the words "feminazi" and "crazy" and "man-hating" got thrown around a lot. There were many comments like, "Oh, better get your coat hanger ready."'

And the institutionalisation and normalisation of misogyny comes from the whole school culture: from the fact that girls often witness female teachers experiencing sexual harassment and abuse from male pupils with little or no action taken in response. I have lost track of the number of women I have spoken to who work in a school environment so abusive that it would not be tolerated across the vast majority of other sectors. Teachers who have been called sluts, slags, whores and cunts by the boys in their charge, who have received rape threats, had photos taken up their skirts and endured boys circulating underground newspapers speculating about their sex lives. Teachers who have begged for support from senior leadership teams, only to be told that the behaviour 'isn't serious enough to warrant punishment' or that it reveals a deficit in the teacher's own disciplinary abilities.

It can be subtle: pupils who leap to their feet when a male teacher ('Sir') comes into the room, but who lounge in their chairs when a female teacher (addressed by her first name) enters. Students who insist on 'checking' a female teacher's answer with a male teacher instead.

As a teacher in a mainstream secondary school, it has always been assumed that continual, low-level sexual harassment from teenage boys was part of the job. When I say 'low level', I am talking about constant sexually inappropriate language; boys being allowed to get away with murder because 'that's how they are used to seeing women be treated' and, on one occasion, a Year 8 boy smacking a female teacher's bottom with a ruler – 'He's too young to know any better' (at age twelve/thirteen!!) . . . One boy I taught, who was in Year 8, would regularly give himself an erection and then call me over to 'help' with his work . . . A Year 11 boy subjected me over a period of about six months to escalating sexually inappropriate language . . . I was on my own with a group of about ten sixteen-year-old boys . . . they started singing 'our lass has got a massive fanny' . . . the reaction from management was: 'This is part of the job and if you can't handle it you are in the wrong profession.' . . . What gets me down is that, over the years, I have witnessed so many occasions when teenage boys could have been called to account for their behaviour, but instead it's been put back on the woman. Whether that's a girl or a female teacher. So these lads are getting the message reinforced that they can behave how the hell they want and, if a woman protests, it's her that's the problem.

The picture is no different at university where there is a silent epidemic of sexual violence. Young women who have been raped are, variously, being pressured to sign non-disclosure agreements, being ordered to return to campus with their rapists, being blamed by the university, being made to endure traumatic and unethical processes that exonerate abusers without examining evidence, being pushed to confront the perpetrators directly in small rooms where they're jovially encouraged to 'bury the hatchet', being told that it's nothing to do with the university if the woman won't go to the police, being assured that there has been an internal investigation and then being refused any information about the results.

Again and again, young women who have experienced sexual violence at university are forced out of education because of a system that utterly and repeatedly fails them. And, once again, at the root of the problem is a system that sees these as separate, shocking incidents. Not a national scourge debilitating female students and devastating their education.

So we learn that these things are somehow just part of life. We adopt coping mechanisms and take precautions and shrink ourselves a little bit. And, when we leave school, along with our scars, we take our learning. The things that we have learned will 'just happen' to women and girls. The way we will be treated if we say anything. The things that we have learned we should be good at and the areas that are off limits to us. The way we are expected to behave and the penalties that will be exacted if we step outside of those boundaries. The knowledge that boys aren't obligated to follow the same rules, that they aren't responsible for their actions. But we are. And we're responsible for theirs, too, in fact. Knowing already that, if we are mistreated, if we are hurt and abused and humiliated, it isn't their fault, not really. It is probably ours.

And perhaps the most consistent lesson we learn, from childhood onwards, is that it is all our own fault. That, if we speak up, we will be blamed and that it is our own weaknesses, bad choices, failings and mistakes that are at the root of our negative experiences. Not misogyny. Not institutionalised sexism. Not male violence.

The hardest part about that assault was when I tried to tell my partner at the time, he grew upset. Not with what had happened to me, but because I had 'put myself in that situation'. I struggle with the rage that I feel about the injustice of being blamed for an attack done to me. But it told me I was right not to report it. Because, even if people believed me, they'd only blame me.

This individualises the problem, from suggesting that women are only raped when they are silly enough to walk alone at night in a short skirt to telling women that they themselves are responsible for their own underrepresentation in politics and business because they simply aren't 'assertive' or ambitious enough. Stereotypes like the 'angry black woman' have an intersectional impact, helping to shut down those who try to protest or who claim that institutional issues are at play.

It's not you

It is incredibly difficult to grow up in a world in which this individualised focus and blame on victims of abuse exists without internalising it.

And it isn't only abuse, but inherently the way in which we see and value different groups of people. When you are educated in a school system that routinely fails to teach students about empire and colonialism, it is more difficult to join the dots between the direct negative experiences of children of colour and the broader sweep of systemic racism. When you live in a society in which so few public spaces are accessible to disabled people, it is easy to buy into widespread narratives that perceive disabled people as disengaged from public life, instead of actively barred from participation by a complete failure at a systemic level. Young LGBTQ children have told me that a complete lack of acknowledgement of the existence of relationships and identities like theirs during relationships and sex education at school made it easier for them to believe pernicious societal myths about there being something wrong or strange about them. And, for girls, growing up in a world that teaches us that we are weaker, less assertive, more

suited to the domestic sphere, worse suited to STEM, has pro-
found effects as well.

What is the impact of all this on us as individuals? Our lives,
our careers, our relationships, even the people we become (or
what we think of as 'who we are')? What does it mean if we are
conditioned into internalising inequality? What does it mean if a
huge number of us are carrying the weight of trauma and abuse
without ever having been granted the right to describe it in those
terms, let alone address it or get meaningful support? And what
might happen if we were able to acknowledge these things, to
allow ourselves the catharsis and the relief of recognising their
impact and perhaps even to begin to heal?

Thousands of Everyday Sexism Project entries suggest that our
early experiences of harassment and abuse can have a long-lasting
legacy. A woman who was suddenly and violently verbally abused
by a man in a public space at the age of eighteen wrote:

> I just wore the abuse, I didn't know how to react or if what had
> happened was even real. I suppose I was in shock. I have often
> felt anxiety in public spaces, especially around how I dress.
> I realised recently, twenty years later, that this incident is one
> of many small violences that have added to this anxiety over
> the years.

Everybody remembers their first time. The girl who was nine
when the men in the dark car shouted at her to come closer with
her 'dick-sucking lips'. The girl who was eight when her mum told
her not to tell such silly stories about her uncle. The girl who was
ten when a hand made its way up her skirt in the playground. The
seven-year-old who was laughed at when she said she wanted to
be an astronaut. The thirteen-year-old who took off her cardigan

at a family wedding and felt shame and confusion when a relative wolf-whistled at her.

But what we might not realise is that these experiences can shape us for ever. These and a million other tiny, seemingly insignificant pinpricks, from gender stereotypes and 'benevolent' sexism to low-level sexual harassment and even sexual assault.

It connects to everything else that happens – to our sense of self, our perception of worth, our safety, our capacity. All the elements of our daily lives that we think are specific to us have their roots in our past and present experiences . . .

'I just prefer to exercise inside.' (A UK poll found that 60 per cent of women had been sexually harassed while running and half of UK women do less exercise outside as the mornings and evenings get darker.)

'I'm just not one of those people who can haggle for a pay rise!' (Men are 23 per cent more likely to ask for a pay rise than women and the majority of women – 57 per cent – have never asked for a pay rise at all.)

'I'm probably not well enough qualified for the job.' (Women tend only to apply for jobs when they meet 100 per cent of the criteria; men tend to apply if they meet just 60 per cent.)

'Perhaps I'm just not presenting my ideas in the right way.' (Nearly two-thirds of women in tech say their ideas are ignored until a man repeats them.)

'I just can't seem to find enough hours in the day.' (On average, women in the UK carry out 60 per cent more unpaid work – childcare, cooking, domestic chores – than men.)

'I'm just not all that comfortable talking about what I want in bed.' (A study found that 91 per cent of men climaxed during their most recent sexual encounter, compared to 64 per cent of women.)

Normalisation breeds acceptance, not only in society but in ourselves.

We're so used to hearing it is our own fault that we start to believe it.

We get so used to it that we stop fighting.

And nobody ever tells us that we have the right to fight in the first place. We think it is just the way things are.

Mort says:

> 'I am not the kind of girl who . . .', 'I would never . . .' are often statements I hear in my clinic. When I hear this I always ask: why? Where does that idea come from? Did someone tell you that you are not able to do those things? What do you feel when you imagine doing those things you say you would never do? Who do you think would judge you most if you did them? We hold many beliefs and ideas that are not our own, they are often shaped by our earliest learning.

She's right. Just look at those statistics. Hell, look at some more . . .

A US study found that women consistently rated their performance on tests lower (46/100) than men (61/100), even when both groups had the same average score. When told that an employer would use their self-evaluation to decide whether to hire them and what to pay them, women still self-promoted less than men.

Just 12.5 per cent of women negotiate for a starting salary, compared with 52 per cent of men.

Women are dramatically more likely than men to be underpaid (they make up two-thirds of workers aged twenty-five and over who are paid less than the minimum wage), but they are much less likely than men to make an official complaint about it.

Data from hundreds of millions of LinkedIn users shows that women apply for 20 per cent fewer jobs and are 16 per cent less likely to apply after viewing a job's requirements. They are also 26 per cent less likely to ask for a referral, even when they have a connection to someone at the hiring company.

It isn't a coincidence, is it? It's not just you; it's not just some character quirk or funny behavioural trait. It is much more statistically significant than that. These are gendered issues on a massive scale. What we tend to explain to ourselves as personal foibles are really systemic barriers.

PATRIARCHY?
WHAT PATRIARCHY?

So the answer is clear: women are their own worst enemies, right? They should just change their behaviour if they want to get ahead. Stop blaming men for everything when this is clearly a huge own-goal. Start speaking up for yourselves in the workplace. Get tough. Assert yourselves. Walk away if someone doesn't treat you right. Ask for that promotion. Don't be put off going into a field if it's what you love, even if there aren't that many other women in it.

Our whole lives, we have been taught to view our challenges, our stumbles and our failures as our own fault. And, at the same time, we have been conditioned by society to ignore, explain away and belittle our experiences of sexism, discrimination and abuse.

We become so used to being taught that we are to blame that we begin to blame ourselves without question. Or, rather, we begin to think this is all just part of who we are.

The promotion you don't feel able to ask for. The unsatisfactory sex you don't have the confidence to address. The way you interact with your male peers. The pay rise you haven't managed to negotiate. All just coincidences. All individual problems. Because there's no such thing as systemic misogyny. No such thing as patriarchy.

The idea that the patriarchy doesn't exist would be a hilarious joke if it weren't for the fact that it makes women's oppression the punchline.

Indeed, this notion is currently having a bit of a renaissance. Think academics selling millions of books and making millions of pounds by suggesting to their millions of young, impressionable, male followers that women don't face any systemic barriers, so any inequality they face must be down to their own faulty biological design and flawed life choices. Sound familiar?

Unsurprisingly, this is proving highly popular among the people who benefit from patriarchy the most. It must be appealing to pat yourself on the back and reassure yourself that it's not your fault that everyone on the board of your company looks just like you; it's just because you guys are, well, *better*. (Hey, your dad putting that call in to his golf mates had nothing to do with it, okay?)

When we use the word 'patriarchy', we are talking about a historical system that has been designed by and for those who have always held the most power in our society: white, wealthy, non-disabled men. A racist, classist, heteronormative, ableist system. We are talking about white supremacy. About male domination. About a hierarchy that has been built into the institutions within which we live our lives – from governments and political structures to workplaces and jobs, education, social norms, welfare and health infrastructure. And we can see the trickle-down effect of this hierarchy at every stage. As women continue to battle for the right to control their own bodies. As black people continue to lose their lives to police violence with near-impunity for the officers who kill them. As broken welfare systems keep families pinned down in poverty while billionaires play with space rockets.

Yes, many things have improved over time – not by accident, but because of the dedicated struggle of campaigners and activists over decades, many of whom have paid for advances in civil rights with their lives. 'Equality of opportunity,' cry the straight, white, non-disabled men earning tens of thousands of pounds a month from their Patreon subscribers. But the structures, the underlying attitudes and many of the systemic barriers remain.

Does this mean that every individual negative outcome experienced by any woman, anywhere, is directly caused by patriarchy? Of course not. A woman might make a terrible mistake at work that costs her her job, just as a man might. And no, it doesn't mean that men aren't immune from bad fortune either. But, collectively, does it play a role in the bigger picture? The fact that women make up the majority of underpaid workers? That they are missing from leadership and political roles? That they're desperately underrepresented across the sectors currently making the decisions and creating the technology that will shape all of our lives in the near future? Damn right it does.

Each of us as individuals has different experiences. Often those experiences will be dictated by our overlapping identities as women, as disabled women, as women of colour, as trans women. And, of course, even within those categories and the overlaps between those categories, each individual's experiences and life events will look different, too. None of us walks an identical path. But all of us are shaped by our experiences. And, if those experiences are influenced by the (heteronormative, racist, classist, ableist) patriarchy, then a lot of the outcomes and realities – from our job to our domestic situation – are likely to be shaped by it, too.

This argument tends to leave those aforementioned academics frothing furiously, decrying that feminists are, once again, trying to turn all women into helpless victims, infantilising them with the argument that their invisible oppression is inescapable and that they must resign themselves to a life of misery and failure. Women will never stand on their own two feet, those guys argue, if we continue to make disempowered, shrinking violets of ourselves.

The trouble with this is that the oppression isn't so invisible after all. Especially if you're living it. Ignorance, in this case, is oppression, not bliss. In reality, it's a hell of a lot more empowering to acknowledge the structures that keep you down than to continue being indoctrinated into believing that it's just your own silly fault. This isn't about absolving women of all personal responsibility or encouraging them not to bother trying. It's about celebrating the successes they've already achieved, in spite of a system designed to work against them, and allowing them to feel righteous anger at the barriers they've faced but not been permitted to name.

Let's say, for example, that you're one of the estimated 54,000 women in the UK who lose their jobs because of maternity discrimination every year. But, of course, your boss has reassured you that it has nothing to do with the fact that you're pregnant. No, that's just a very unfortunate coincidence; it was your performance that slipped unacceptably, you see.

Yet the chances are that all 54,000 of you didn't cock up your job at the same time. It kind of feels like there has to be something else going on here, right?

The argument of 'equality of opportunity' relies almost entirely

on deliberately and cynically ignoring deep-seated, systemic inequalities. The problem is: many of us are already programmed to
do this because we are so used to these inequalities that we don't
really think about them any more.

Imagine that a woman and her male partner both started a new
job in the same year and were supposed to work the same hours,
but were also required to split between them a third, voluntary
position, which they would have to fit around their paid employment. We would immediately cry foul if the man suggested she
take on the vast majority of the volunteering, leaving him unfairly
advantaged in finding the time to progress in his primary career.
This would seem unfair and, if the man subsequently became
more successful at work, we would immediately point to the
discrepancy in their extra hours as the reason for his superior
achievement.

However, this is the precise situation in which the vast majority
of working women in heterosexual relationships in the UK find
themselves. On average, when a heterosexual couple co-habit in
the UK, women do approximately sixteen hours of household
chores a week, while men do six. During the COVID-19 lockdown, mothers spent 77 per cent more time on childcare than
fathers. But, instead of pointing out the absurdity of expecting
women to magically manage a 'third shift' of childcare, house-
work and emotional labour alongside their paid work without
being disadvantaged in comparison to their male partners, we
simply shrug our shoulders and say, 'It's not our fault women don't
perform as well as men.'

Nor is it simply a case of women needing to 'get a grip' and
demand their partners share the chores: the inequality is often
structurally ingrained by systems and policies that subtly reinforce it. Men in the UK are offered a paltry two weeks of statutory

paternity leave, compared to the thirty-nine weeks of statutory maternity pay. And the inherent flaws in the shared parental leave system mean that it is simply not a viable financial option for a huge number of families.

What if none of it was ever you? What if it was always the system? A system that relies on its own invisibility for its preservation. A system that maintains this invisibility in the neatest, most insidious deception, by convincing women to believe that they themselves are to blame.

When we see women performing less well than men across various different metrics in the professional world, our response is invariably to try to 'fix' the women. Networking sessions, mentoring, women's groups, assertiveness courses – the list of supposedly brilliant 'solutions' for women to engage with grows by the day. But rarely do we stop to correlate these 'fixes' with the prejudice and discrimination women face.

Women aren't the problem; the system is.

That same LinkedIn study – the one that revealed how women are less likely to put themselves forward for jobs – also showed that recruiters are 13 per cent less likely to click on a woman's profile than a man's. Research has repeatedly shown that, when identical CVs are sent to recruiters with 'male-' or 'female-sounding' names, recruiters rate the 'male' applicants as significantly more competent and hireable, offer them a higher starting salary and extend more career-mentoring opportunities to them. Studies have revealed similar outcomes with 'white-sounding' and 'non-white-sounding' names and resumes.

One in eight HR decision-makers say that they are reluctant to hire women who may go on to have children; almost a third of young women report sex discrimination while working or looking for work; and one in five is paid less than her male colleagues for the same or similar employment. In 2017, black women in the US earned 61 cents for every dollar earned by white men, amounting to $23,653 less in earnings over an entire year. In the span of a forty-year career, this translates into an average lifetime earnings gap of $946,120 between black women and white men. A TUC poll found that nearly one in three disabled workers (already paid 20 per cent less than their non-disabled peers) was treated unfairly at work during the COVID-19 pandemic. These problems are not individual, but structural.

It's all very well suggesting that women don't put themselves forward for political office, but placing the blame on the unwillingness of potential candidates not only obscures the valid, systemic reasons for that reluctance (from media misogyny to rape and death threats), but also masks the reality of the institutional barriers they face. Recent research from the Fawcett Society found that 'women face obstacles at every stage on the way to parliament, particularly from "gatekeepers" within the political parties . . . Women still meet resistance from local parties who have a preconceived idea of their "ideal candidate", who is white, male, middle-class and able-bodied.' Two pregnant women in the study were deselected and another woman candidate was told by local councillors: 'We just need to get anyone else to stand, we can't have a young woman, we can't.'

Then there's the fact that the Reykjavík Index, which assesses public attitudes towards female leadership across the G7 countries, repeatedly shows that just 78 per cent of people are comfortable with the idea of a female head of government.

And one or two women breaking through isn't enough to fix the attitude problem. In Germany, in spite of Angela Merkel's long-term chancellorship, just 41 per cent of people said they felt very comfortable with a woman as head of government.

The idea of equality of opportunity only holds up if you don't stop to look too closely. As soon as you do, it all tumbles down like a house of cards. It's not just the overt discrimination, unconscious bias, sexual harassment and abuse. It's also the fact that the institutions themselves are already rigged in ways that work to maintain and renew the cycle of inequality.

Let's take a look, for example, at the people with decision-making power in our overwhelmingly white, male, privately educated parliament – membership of which, the academic dudebros would have us believe, is entirely based on who is courageous enough to run and talented enough to succeed.

Except . . .

In the House of Lords, where a group of unelected lawmakers take part in political decision-making, with the ability to examine and reject bills and to impact our lives in enormous ways. Indeed, twenty-six of those seats are reserved for Church of England bishops – and you might not be shocked to learn that just five of those twenty-six are women. (You can't really argue that it's just because women weren't plucky enough to go for the role either, given that the church banned them from becoming bishops until 2013.) Then there are ninety-two hereditary peers – people who have political power over our country and our lives purely because of the family they were born into. And guess what? The vast majority of those peerages can only be passed down to sons, not daughters. Because patriarchy. So straight away, in one fell swoop, you've just essentially cordoned off a massive 'male-only' area in our supposedly egalitarian, un-patriarchal political system. You know how many of our MPs and our cabinet ministers were educated at Oxbridge? Around a fifth. How many went to private school? Almost a third. You know what proportion of the population that particular recruitment pool represents? Seven per cent. And, before you say that those people who went to state schools just aren't trying hard enough, look at the research: studies show that privileged, white men are likely to recruit in their own image. Hell, even Nancy Astor – that pioneering first female MP we're so often encouraged to celebrate as a beacon of feminist courage and progress – only got her seat because she took it over from her husband when he was bumped up to the House of Lords. Not exactly a route to power that was available to 99.9 per cent of women. Then throw in a recent investigation that revealed donors wealthy enough to pay more than £3 million to the Conservative Party 'appear to be guaranteed a peerage'. So it's not quite as simple as 'equality of opportunity' in the end, is it?

Even when women *do* act in the way people suggest – trying to be more assertive, standing up for themselves, negotiating and generally behaving 'more like men' – studies repeatedly find that they are punished for it. Because 'fixing' the women doesn't change the unfair system they are operating within, which still finds a way to disadvantage them.

Men who exhibit anger at work, for example, receive a boost in their perceived status, whereas women who express anger in the same context are accorded lower status and lower wages and seen as less competent. A woman's perceived deserved compensation drops by 35 per cent, twice as much as a man's, when both are equally aggressive in workplace communications. Women are also dramatically more likely than men to be punished for showing assertive behaviours (e.g. asking for a raise or talking more during a meeting) or for initiating negotiations in the workplace. And high-achieving women are far more likely than their male peers to be described as 'abrasive' in their performance reviews.

Almost never does anyone stop to say: hang on a minute, maybe there's a reason that women are performing less strongly in a system set up by and for white men. Rarely does anybody wonder what would happen if we chose to change the system instead. When they do, they tend to be outliers. People who have themselves experienced systemic prejudice. Like Ellen Pao, who simply did away with salary negotiation altogether during her tenure as CEO at Reddit, replacing it with fixed starting rates. This circumvented the initial bartering process in which men are more likely to play hardball and women are penalised for the same behaviour, thereby instigating a gender pay gap right from the outset. It was a rare example of changing the system instead of blaming the women. And it isn't a coincidence that it was pioneered by Pao, who had herself sued her former employer, a venture capital firm, for gender discrimination. (Pao lost the case, but succeeded in starting an important conversation about the unequal treatment of women in tech.)

And what happened to Pao, who also took action to end revenge pornography and ban Reddit communities that had become synonymous with harassment and abuse? Oh yes, she ended up resigning after hundreds of thousands of Reddit users signed petitions calling for her to be ousted. She was also referred to as 'a manipulative individual who will sue her way to the top' and a 'bitch', with some users fantasising about punching her in the face and starting subreddits with names like 'EllenPaoIsaBigCunt'. It was significant, given that just one in 285 Asian American women working in tech is an executive, that the wording of the petition signed by so many of Reddit's substantially white-male dominated users accused her of 'overstep[ping] her boundaries'. At the time Pao left Reddit, a subreddit called 'raping women' remained active. This really says everything about power, priorities and progress.

As Gloria Steinem simply and powerfully puts it: 'Women do not have the power to be our own worst enemies.'

The sleight of hand here is that we have changed our rhetoric without changing the system. We have started talking about empowered women in politics without actually doing anything to change the archaic political system in which they operate. We have started talking about women 'having it all' without shifting the societal expectations that see them shouldering all the domestic work and without fixing the broken structures that see their careers impacted by maternity leave. We are expecting women somehow, magically, to contort themselves into ever more demanding and ridiculous shapes in order to manage every spinning plate. But it is women who are having to adapt, to change, to spread themselves thinner and thinner. The system isn't morphing or adjusting to facilitate any of this. And the attitudes have barely changed at all. In 1920, MP Nancy Astor addressed her male peers in her maiden speech: 'I do not want you to look on your lady member as a fanatic or a lunatic.' In 2021, when Stella Creasy tried to go into parliament to do her job with her baby in a sling, she noted on Instagram that she was confronted by a police officer who told her not to think she could just go anywhere she wanted 'as if she was an MP'. And these ideas are not just confined to politics. It was only in 2015 that Nobel Prize-winning scientist Tim Hunt spoke at a major scientific conference: 'Let me tell you about my trouble with girls . . . three things happen when they are in the lab . . . You fall in love with them, they fall in love with you and, when you criticise them, they cry.'

Keeping us down

Because we see all this as 'normal', just a snapshot of the world around us, the way it is, we don't stop to consider the impact it has on women's lives and on their mental health. One in eight American women experiences depression in her lifetime – twice the rate of men. Research in 2020 found that 30 per cent of women in the UK aged between eighteen and twenty-four suffered from anxiety – double the percentage of men. And it isn't difficult to find evidence that this poor mental health might be impacted by the extra, invisible load society expects women to shoulder. During the pandemic, when lockdowns resulted in women massively increasing the amount of unpaid care and domestic chores they were undertaking while, in many cases, simultaneously trying to keep their careers afloat (not to mention those stuck at home with abusive partners), research repeatedly showed a burgeoning crisis in women's mental health: 27 per cent of women reported increases in challenges in relation to their mental health, compared to 10 per cent of men.

When we don't acknowledge that the problem exists, we leave women to suffer the consequences alone.

Nowhere is this trajectory of harm and pain more heartbreakingly clear than in the hundreds of thousands of stories shared with the Everyday Sexism Project.

One woman, who had been raped twice, wrote: 'I still can't wash away the uncleanness, pain and lost years. I cannot be in a relationship and avoid medical procedures. I don't want anyone near me . . . I hate being like this when I have so much life I want to live.'

But, while sexual violence impacts millions of women and can cause massive and long-lasting trauma, there is trauma, too, in the experiences that are even more common: the normality of being casually seen as less-than; the sting of low-level sexism from within your own family; the constant, throbbing ache of danger in public spaces and the way you subtly find yourself absorbing that sense of fear and vigilance into your daily existence.

Susan Quilliam, a relationship therapist and expert in the psychology of relationships, says: 'The ongoing trauma of the everyday sexism is something that we hardly even notice and, when we do, we don't label it as trauma. And it is trauma . . . It's an ongoing trauma that is not recognised in society.'

How we love

From the relationships we have with our family in childhood to the ones we form later in our lives, the seeds of inequality sown in our early years can go on to blossom into unequal, unfulfilling partnerships and sex lives. But, here again, the ubiquity of gender stereotypes and prescribed gender roles can prevent us from seeing what is oppressive or unfair, even when it is happening right in front of us.

> The idea that we have some kind of sexual obligation to men from the moment we enter puberty is ridiculous and dangerous, but I felt like this for a long time. I sometimes still wonder about my motivation to have sex. I love sex, but I hate the feeling that any sexually charged situation gives me; like I am responsible for the feelings I aroused and therefore have an obligation to fix it.

When we grow up in families in which women take on the bulk of domestic chores, cooking, emotional labour (remembering birthdays, organising social meetups, writing thank-you cards) and unpaid care work, it is easy to replicate that in our own adulthood without stopping to question the unfair distribution of toil. Once again, we tend to individualise, to make excuses for why things have just 'worked out this way'. 'It just makes more sense for me to do the childcare.' 'He just hates hoovering.' 'It's just easier to do it myself than to teach him how.'

> Because he does see that he needs to share the workload with me, he will clean or prepare a meal (from time to time), but I always have to tell him what to do. In this respect, I'm the house manager, organising our home life on my own and enlisting my partner's 'help', rather than working with him on an equal level . . . My children will grow up seeing their mother running the show at home and, even though the world wants to convince them that women and men can share the responsibilities equally, the fact of the matter is, more often than not, we don't.

When our childhoods are suffused with Disney princesses and fairy-tale endings (in which the ultimate success for girls is painted as meeting their handsome prince) and when we are pressured into viewing heterosexual marriage as the pinnacle of achievement (by a society that depends on such marriages for the unpaid labour that keeps their economies turning), then it is easy to internalise the message that finding and keeping a man is more important than how that man makes us feel or the other possible lives we could be living.

When we have spent our lives living in a world in which sexual harassment and abuse are, for many, a near-daily occurrence, it becomes easy to mistake the bare minimum of human decency for great kindness and generosity. Easy to live unequally. To offer more than we receive. To be grateful for what we should expect without question.

It doesn't help that we live in a society that sees a man who changes a nappy as a saint, a boyfriend who occasionally makes brunch as a diamond in the rough, an emotionally supportive man as a rare treasure, yet expects all these things from female partners as a matter of course.

And the normalised experiences of sexism and harassment most of us face from childhood can have an impact on our adult relationships that we might not even be able to recognise. 'We end up not able to trust others and we end up not able to trust ourselves,' Quilliam says. 'We don't trust ourselves to know what we want in sex or in a relationship, we don't trust ourselves to listen to "that was wrong" and we don't trust ourselves to listen to "that was right" . . . There is a lack of safety for women around relationships that is often constant, permanent and unconscious.'

When we grow up bombarded with messages about male sexual domination and female submission, when pornography teaches us that sex is an aggressive, powerful thing done by men to women with the purpose of meeting men's 'needs', when women who know what they want in bed are parodied as harsh dominatrix types or disapprovingly portrayed as unacceptably promiscuous, we learn that it isn't feminine to speak up about what we want in bed, to have bold needs and desires, or to expect men to satisfy them.

When I ask Quilliam whether our societal norms about sex (such as assumptions about men's sex drive being higher or the idea that it isn't appropriate for women to talk about being unsatisfied in bed), she is unequivocal. 'It's deeper than that. We teach women that they shouldn't question what they want: they shouldn't [even] find out what they want' – let alone have the confidence to articulate that to someone else.

She points out that penetrative sex is seen as 'standard' in heterosexual couples and women have to measure their desires against this so-called 'standard', even if it fails to work for them physiologically. In other words, in a society that presents us with a male-centric, heteronormative vision of what sex is, it is all too easy for that to become internalised and to manifest itself in unsatisfying sexual relationships that prioritise men's desires over women's pleasure. A study of over 2,300 women found that only 57 per cent usually have orgasms when they engage in sex with a heterosexual partner, compared to 95 per cent of men and 75 per cent for lesbian women.

Here, too, there are unavoidable connections. Connections with a $12 billion global pornography industry that commodifies women's bodies for men's profit, that warps young people's ideas of what sex looks like, that overlaps with and knowingly profits from the colossal problem of human trafficking and modern slavery. An industry with an impact so massive, particularly in the absence of alternative healthy information provided to young people about respectful relationships and sexual consent, that its legacy echoes across the lives and relationships of millions of people. And, because it is an industry that produces and maintains misogynistic, racist, ableist norms, it becomes another part of the system that helps to ingrain those forms of oppression in our daily lives and our most intimate experiences.

My former husband had seen porn where a man basically fucked a woman's breasts and came on her face. One night, without warning, he suddenly sat on my diaphragm, jammed my breasts together around his erection and began chanting about how he wanted to come between my tits. I was terrified – he wasn't in good shape, but he was much stronger than I was and outweighed me by about 40–50 pounds – and could barely breathe, but, when I told him I couldn't breathe and tried to bat his hands away, he just kept chanting the same thing. I somehow managed to turn my head so he couldn't come on my face, but it was a near thing. Afterwards, he rolled over and went to sleep and I had to clean up the mess by myself. The next day, I tried to talk to him about it, but he denied it had ever happened. It took me nearly twenty years to realise I'd been raped.

Bodies

For many of us, seeing women's bodies co-opted by a patriarchal, racist, ageist, capitalist system as objectified commodities for men to purchase and control will also have a massive impact on our perception of our own bodies, although, as with all the different forms of misogyny that are so normalised in our society, we may not realise that this is the source of our body image struggles. If we do, we may still not know how to move past these struggles.

We are bombarded every day with hundreds of images of women's nearly naked bodies, all conforming to unattainable and unrealistic beauty standards that imply white-skinned, emaciated, large-breasted, long-blonde-haired, young, heavily made-up, non-disabled, hairless women should be the pinnacle of human desire and success. The negative and destructive relationship with our own bodies that this forcibly creates for many women will last a lifetime. It will drain our finances, our head space, our confidence, our time, our energy. It will deny us simple pleasure in food, exercise, clothes, social activities, uninhibited sex. It will warp our relationship with ourselves and with other people. It will affect the way we value ourselves and the way other people value us and the way we believe we deserve to be valued. It will prevent us accessing healthcare. Its impact on our lives may be enormous. And we may never realise it at all. Because the world tells us, once again, that it is all just part of who we are. Insecure. Obsessed with your tummy. Self-loathing. Ashamed of being menopausal.

Mort says: 'The media's constant policing of female bodies means many of us are distracted from living the lives we truly wish to lead as we chase the unattainable beauty standards set out in our society, which say we must be one size, shape, age and so on.'

And we will become so used to it – the shame, the worry, the daily work we do to try to control and mitigate our bodies, the hours of grooming we believe to be 'necessary', the constant internal chatter of self critique, the idea that we are not fully worthy of love, that our value is measured by the number on the scales or the gap between our thighs – that we won't even notice it any more. It will just be another weight we will carry with us. And, if we do notice it at all, we will, once again, blame ourselves. We will think of this societal-inflicted trauma as personal quirks and failings. We will think it is all our own fault.

It is necessary to keep us this way. To keep us locked in, blaming ourselves, uncommunicating and in the dark about the true scale of the injustice that affects our lives every day. It allows us to continue propping up a completely unjust system that thrives because of our subjugation and unpaid labour. If we start to join the dots and realise that this is connected to a world in which we are seen as second-class citizens, a world in which our bodies are public property for sexual harassment, in which we are not afforded the dignity and the power to make our own decisions about what we choose to do with our own reproductive organs, in which we are expected to allow ourselves to be sexualised for other people's profits but shamed when we enjoy our own sexuality, in which we are underpaid and underrepresented and exploited and oppressed and abused, then we might just revolt. Against all of it. And that would be a disaster for the system. A disaster for the white men who run it and benefit from it.

Nor is any of this particularly under the radar. Patriarchal control of women's bodies and policing of their sex lives is so normalised that it is even celebrated. As I write, Peter Andre tweets a photograph of his daughter Princess in her school uniform with the caption: 'Now, about becoming a nun . . .' The post is flooded with admiring comments about what a great dad he is and how sweet the sentiment is.

*

Normalisation looks different in different contexts. For some women, we are told it is about 'choice'. For others, 'culture'. In every case, we will find a way to disguise the reality, which is an imbalance of power.

Dr Leyla Sirad Hussein OBE is a psychotherapist and social activist who has spent decades working to end violence against women and girls. As a prominent activist against female genital mutilation (FGM), she has spoken powerfully about the importance of recognising FGM as part of the spectrum of violence against women, rather than ring-fencing it off into a 'cultural' silo. FGM is the deliberate cutting or injury of female genitals or the removal of external female genitalia for no medical reason. Most often practised on girls and young women under eighteen years of age, 200 million girls and women alive today have undergone FGM.

'Tackling FGM has been treated as a solo issue, like it was a separate thing,' Hussein explains. It's not . . . It's about controlling women's bodies. It's to control female sexuality. That's the reason it's done. I'm sick and tired of hearing this is religious culture: that's not why girls are being mutilated, butchered.'

She points out striking similarities between FGM and cosmetic labiaplasty, which she was shocked to discover was legal in the UK. Cosmetic labiaplasty is surgery to reduce the size or change the appearance of the labia minora for no medical reason. Hussein began to speak to white women who had elected to have the procedure. One was afraid her partner would leave her for a younger woman. Another said that 'it needs to be trimmed so it can be pretty'.

'What do [those] who [uphold] FGM say?' Hussein asks, shaking her head. '[You] need to have a tight vagina for [your] future husband . . . so pretty much the same exact reasoning. These two women come from a patriarchal system. But, if that woman is white, it's "labiaplasty". It's not barbaric any more.' Women are told that labiaplasty can help their 'mental wellbeing', Hussein says, 'instead of teaching girls from an early age that actually vaginas are all different, [unlike in] porn'. She points to figures showing that labiaplasty is the fastest-growing form of cosmetic surgery in the UK, with operations increasing five-fold in the decade to 2013 and 200 NHS operations carried out on girls under eighteen in 2015–16 alone, 150 of them under fifteen. She laughs in disbelief. 'Wait a minute, so [what is happening to] this fifteen-year-old girl is barbaric, but *this* one is going to make a choice?'

Fundamentally, she says, this is about a society 'telling girls early on there's something wrong with their bodies'. It is about the patriarchal oppression of women and girls. The blind spots in our utterly disjointed responses to these issues show how closely white supremacy and patriarchy are intertwined. 'You cannot talk about race without talking about gender. It's just not going to work because it's connected.' She demonstrates this with a succinct summary of her own experience: 'I was cut because I was born a female. And the reason I never got justice is because the system I live under said because I was black and my family were . . .' she trails off. As of September 2021, just one person in the UK has ever been convicted of FGM. Hussein was contacted by a white woman who, at the age of thirteen, told her parents she was a lesbian. Her father took a blade to her genitalia. 'Why? Because he thought the clitoris was how she would enjoy women. He thought, "I'm going to damage this." It's about controlling female sexuality. Do you see how similar the reasoning is?' That man, she says, was eventually convicted of crimes relating to child abuse, neglect and sexual assault. 'But, if she looked like me, there's a whole different [set] of policies and laws in place.'

She continues:

> This is violence. Don't call it tradition. Don't call it culture.
> Language is such a powerful tool. To me, cultural tradition is
> food, dancing, the dress I wear. But, if you call one of the most
> horrific experiences of my life culture, that's offensive and racist.
> If it was white women or white girls, you just wouldn't. We need
> to acknowledge that we are still living in a society that upholds a
> patriarchal system. And it's racist.

When Nimco Ali, another anti-FGM campaigner, told her teacher in Manchester at the age of seven that she had been taken abroad during the school holidays and undergone FGM, her teacher told her it was 'a bit like a bar mitzvah'.

So labiaplasty is described as an 'individual choice'; FGM is called a 'cultural issue'. Victims of domestic abuse are blamed for not leaving; rape survivors find their clothing and behaviour scrutinised – no matter how absurd such determined focus in the wrong direction seems.

Blaming women or calling their systematic oppression an

'individual choice' is so much easier than recognising that an entire society – its norms, its political structures, its systems of justice and law enforcement – is deeply flawed in ways that uphold and worsen inequality and hamper efforts to fight it. It is much easier than acknowledging that there are tens of thousands of men committing deliberate, criminal acts of violence every year and going completely unpunished.

It feels safer to blame the women because then we can keep a handle on the problem. If the women cause it, it's nobody else's responsibility to fix. If the women cause it, the system is okay. If it's women's fault, we can all feel reassured that justice is available to us, comfortable in the knowledge that those who do all the right things will be protected and vindicated. If the women are to blame, we don't need to overhaul our institutions, root out ingrained, structural problems or, crucially, ask anything of men.

Instead of recognising these structural problems we need to fix, we continue to think of women's rape, murder, assault and harassment as one-offs. Products of individual choices. Separate, distinct problems. Isolated incidents.

'ISOLATED INCIDENTS'

'Two men have been arrested on suspicion of murder after the body of a woman was found at a house. Initial inquiries suggested she had been stabbed multiple times. Detective Chief Inspector Cheryl Chatterton said officers were treating it as an "isolated" incident.'

*

'A forty-year-old man who was arrested on suspicion of murder following the death of a woman at an address in St Ives yesterday (22 February) has been detained. Detective Inspector Dale Mepstead said: "I would like to reassure the public that we believe this is an isolated incident."'

*

'The woman aged in her seventies was sadly found dead . . . Detective Chief Inspector Chris Friday from the Surrey and

Sussex Major Crime Unit said: "This is being treated as a tragic isolated incident.'"

*

Isolated incidents. Shocking. Tragic. Unpredictable. Unpreventable.

But, when something happens once every three days, it isn't an isolated incident. And that's how often women are murdered by men in the UK. Worldwide, 137 women are killed by a family member *every single day*. These are not isolated incidents. They are the opposite. And the opposite of an isolated incident is a pattern.

3 March 2020. A young woman has gone missing in Clapham. Her name is Sarah Everard. Over the next few days, photographs of her fill our laptop screens and newspaper columns – her kind, beautiful smile beaming out everywhere. News websites share a photograph of everything she was wearing on the day she disappeared. A green rain jacket. Navy-blue trousers with a white diamond pattern. Turquoise and orange trainers. Green earphones and a white woolly hat. Just days later, her remains are discovered in woodland in Ashford, Kent.

People are shocked. How could this happen to a woman in the UK in 2021? There is outrage, grief, wall-to-wall media coverage. Sarah is on the front page of almost every major national newspaper, as well as featuring across the international media. 'Sarah Everard: missing woman's case sends UK into shock.' Her disappearance is a grotesque and shocking aberration.

Except it wasn't.

Sarah's death was a horrible tragedy, devastating to her family and friends and rightly mourned by the general public. But it wasn't an aberration at all.

The day before Sarah disappeared, a woman named Samantha Heap was found dead at a house in Congleton, Cheshire. A man was later charged with her murder. The case didn't make the front pages. The day after Sarah went missing, Geetika Goyal was found dying of stab wounds on a Leicester pavement. A man was later charged with her murder. The case apparently didn't warrant many headlines. On the same day, Imogen Bohajczuk was found dead at a property in Oldham, her body so badly mutilated that she had to be identified by dental records. The case didn't make the national news until several months later when her boyfriend was found guilty of having murdered her and then written 'it was me' on her leg in nail varnish. Even then, the coverage was muted, largely confined to a few local papers and a brief article on the BBC News website. The day after that, a teenage girl, Wenjing Lin, was found dead in Rhondda, Wales. Two men were arrested, one on suspicion of murder. Very few people heard about it. Before the month was out, at least eight more women were killed and men then charged with their murders.

In April that year, a further fourteen women would be killed by men. In May, Susan Booth, Maya Zulfiquar, Maria Rawlings, Chenise Gregory, Agnes Akom, Wendy Cole, Svetlana Mihalachi, Nicola Kirk, Agita Geslere, Lauren Wilson, Peninah Kabeba, Jill Hickery and Bethany Vincent would die. Have you ever heard any of their names?

You almost certainly haven't. Doesn't that seem completely bizarre? That women are dying in their hundreds and we almost never hear about it?

It isn't a coincidence that you haven't heard their names. One in four women in the UK will experience domestic abuse and 85,000 a year will experience rape or attempted rape. We live within a system that normalises and smooths these incidents away. A police force that often records them incorrectly and sometimes even sneers at the victims. A political elite that fails to see them as part of a broader crisis. A media that often presents those who come forward as opportunistic and promiscuous when it covers their stories at all. A society that privileges some victims over others because of the way it values and ranks women, making it even less likely that some stories will be heard. A culture that blames the women for asking for it and provoking their own attacks. A justice system that lets 98.6 per cent of perpetrators off the hook, even after they've been reported to the police.

And you can see it happening in real time. The machinery creaks into action to minimise, dismiss and soothe. Don't worry your pretty little heads. Don't join the dots. What did she do wrong? Isolated incidents. Extremely rare. Tragic. Bad apple. Wrong 'un. Every single aspect of our response to sexual- and gender-based violence replicates and strengthens the systemic conditions that enable it to happen in the first place. And it continues to render the scale and the interconnected nature of the problem invisible to us, leaving systemic solutions completely out of reach.

In the days after Sarah Everard's disappearance, women in Clapham told reporters that police officers were knocking on their doors warning them not to go out alone. The stage was set. From the very beginning, the messaging from those whose job it is to keep us safe was clear: this is on *women*. Women should be more careful. You are responsible for avoiding your own rape or murder. Nobody was knocking on doors telling men and boys they should avoid going outside until the police had pinpointed which of them had done this. (And yes, statistics showed it was overwhelmingly likely to have been a male perpetrator.) Nobody was saying, 'Until we sort this out, maybe we should keep all the men in after dark, just to be safe. Just common sense, isn't it?' Because what we call common sense, in these cases, is anything but. It is just further absorption of the messages we've already received from childhood. 'Lock up your daughters,' they shout gleefully when a chubby, cute little boy toddles around next to the cherubic girls at playgroup. But do we ever stop to think about what that actually means? Some twenty years later, those little baby girls might get a knock on the door from the police telling them exactly that. Lock yourselves up. Keep yourselves safe, shut away, restrained. Because male violence is inevitable. There's nothing we can do about that. But we can police you instead.

This narrative was echoed online, where the following phrases trended on Twitter for days:

'She was just walking home'

'She did all the right things'

'#NotAllMen'

Women learn what the 'right things' are very, very early. Once, I was doing a workshop with 13–14-year-old pupils in a lovely school in a little rural town with cobbled streets and overpriced gift shops. Amid conversations about advertising and role-modelling, I asked the pupils to guess how their lives might be different if they were a different sex. I expected light-hearted answers about hobbies, perhaps, or clothing, which I could use to reflect on the sexism of advertising and gender roles. Instead, a girl tentatively raised her hand and said these exact words: 'You wouldn't have to be scared all the time.' And, when I asked if other girls felt the same way, every single hand in the class was raised. They started to share their stories of leaving school early in the winter months to get home before dark, of switching schedules to be able to walk in pairs, of gripping their hockey sticks tightly in their hands in anticipation of potential attackers. They were thirteen years old. And already they had learned that they would be expected to protect themselves. Already they had adopted many of the coping mechanisms and safety measures adopted by generations of women before them.

Things women do to keep 'safe' on a daily basis:

- Carry keys between your fingers in case you need to use them as a weapon
- Cross the street to avoid large groups of men
- Take a longer route to avoid badly lit or wooded areas
- Change your commute or route to school to avoid an area in which you've previously been harassed
- Switch to exercising indoors or give up exercise altogether after outdoor harassment
- Record a man's voice on your answering machine to give the impression you don't live alone
- Wear a fake wedding ring
- Carry some kind of weapon, such as pepper spray, a knife or even aerosol deodorant
- Always let someone know where you are going
- Use an app to send your tracking location to a friend or partner
- Always text girl friends to let each other know you've got home safely
- Go to the bathroom in groups
- Dance in groups
- Watch your drink like a hawk and cover it with your hand
- Carry a whistle or rape alarm
- Check and double-check that the cab you're taking is licensed
- Change your clothing to avoid harassment
- Wear headphones, even with no music playing, to try to fend off unwanted advances

- Don't wear headphones so you'll be able to hear someone approaching from behind
- Wear flat shoes in case you need to run
- Wear your hair in a ponytail so you attract less unwanted attention
- Don't wear your hair in a ponytail in case it provides someone with an easy way to grab you
- Don't turn your back on boys in a school corridor
- Stand against the wall in the playground at break time

It can be a real shock for people to read that list. For women, it may be shocking to see so many of the things that are second nature to you written down together like this. Shocking to realise that you aren't alone: that other women are doing these things, too. Shocking to see the list in this context and to begin to recognise that this isn't just you being a bit 'paranoid' or nervy. That it is the result of growing up in a world in which you've learned, through experience, to fear for your safety pretty much all the time; a world that has socialised you to believe that the person responsible for fixing this frankly outrageous reality is you. Shocking to discover that you have been living in a fairly constant state of hyper-vigilance for so long that you have ceased even to recognise it as anything out of the ordinary.

For most men, the list is often shocking for a different reason. The realisation that they have rarely, if ever, thought about taking these measures. The shock of learning that the women they love and care about in their lives do all this and more on a day-to-day basis.

A boy I knew from uni used to talk about how he loved walking outside at night, just by himself. He could walk for hours in deserted streets under the stars and even watched the sunrise a few times. The joy and serenity he spoke of made me so envious that I nearly teared up. When he asked me why I didn't do the same, I knew he didn't understand at all. I'm a woman.

It is a constant, exhausting performance that must be renewed each day, designed to fend off the inevitable. But it isn't designed to keep us safe from threat, not really.

In 2021, a spate of reports suggested a deeply concerning new trend of young women being 'spiked' while on nights out, usually in clubs and bars. But, rather than the original use of the term 'spiked' to describe the covert addition of drugs like Rohypnol to a victim's drink, the term was now being used, horribly, to describe the injection of unwitting victims with a needle and syringe. The reports continued to pour in from across the UK, beginning to suggest not a series of shocking isolated incidents, but a new, quite widespread tactic being adopted and proliferated by predators.

At this point, it must have occurred to many of us who grew up solemnly nodding as we were instructed always to watch our drinks and never to remove our hands from the tops of our glasses that perhaps the time had come to stop training us to take preventative individual action because it clearly didn't work. I wonder whether the next generation will be encouraged to go out dressed in full-body armour or perhaps a fetching suit of very fine chainmail. Or whether we might, finally, belatedly, logically, begin to address the broader, structural problem of men attacking women instead.

We carry on with these behaviours even though we all know somebody who has been attacked and abused in spite of them. We carry on – partly because, even then, even as women die around us, there's nothing else. Nobody is doing anything else to protect us. Nobody is stopping the men from doing the killing. But we also carry on for another reason – perhaps the main reason. We perform these behaviours because we are performing our virtue: showing that we do not deserve to be attacked. And, perhaps without even realising, we are already working to shield ourselves from the decision that we deserved what we got. That we were asking for it. That we weren't careful enough.

When 'she was just walking home' and 'she did all the right things' trend online, they tell us exactly what our society thinks about women who fall victim to male violence: that some of them have the right to be mourned. Those who were good girls. Those who were perfect victims. Those who were sweet and pretty and innocent and careful and didn't stray off the path or talk to the wolf.

'She was just going for a run', thousands of people tweeted, after 23-year old primary school teacher Ashling Murphy was murdered in Tullamore, Ireland, in January 2022. As if that was what made it unbearable. Not the overwhelming tragedy of her death, but the fact that she hadn't stepped outside the lines. She had done nothing to ask for it.

What if she hadn't done all the right things? What if she hadn't just been walking home? What if she hadn't just been going for a run?

What if she were partying at two o'clock in the morning, passed out in an alleyway in a short skirt? What if she were on her way to meet a married lover or chose to take a shortcut through the woods? What if she had been drunk or on drugs or waiting to meet a man who would pay to have sex with her?

Would that have made us less willing to mourn? Would we have been less inclined to profess our public grief and demand justice? Would she have been less likely to appear on the front pages of our national newspapers? Precedent would suggest that yes, it would.

And that's the system. It's okay to mourn one or two high-profile deaths when they fit into the wider system of women's training to behave, to keep themselves tightly locked up, never to step outside the lines. But, even in our mourning, we are reinforcing the rules, tightening the restraints around the rest of the women, reminding ourselves of the tiny circle of space we must confine ourselves to if we would like our deaths to be seen as a tragedy.

The perfect victim

The vast majority of women's deaths at the hands of men go unreported and largely unremarked-upon. Unless the victim is young, white and beautiful (think Reeva Steenkamp on the front page of the tabloids in her bikini the morning after she'd been shot dead, with a headline that didn't even mention her name), nobody is particularly interested.

Less than a year before Sarah's death, sisters Bibaa Henry and Nicole Smallman were celebrating Bibaa's birthday in a park in Wembley when they were stabbed to death by a man named Danyal Hussein. After they disappeared, their mother, Mina Smallman, said the police seemed 'uninterested' and she was frustrated by a 'lack of urgency' in searching for her daughters. 'I said to the police: "We don't know if there's been foul play here – we have no idea. We are now thirty-six hours on and they haven't turned up,"' she told BBC News the following year. 'I knew instantly why they didn't care. They didn't care because they looked at my daughter's address and they thought they knew who she was. A black woman who lives on a council estate.' Eventually, it was Nicole's partner who found the sisters' bodies, two days later, in the same park where they had been stabbed.

In the aftermath of Sarah Everard's death, Ms Smallman pointed out that there had not been similar interest, immediate large-scale police response and political attention when her own daughters had gone missing and then been found dead. 'They didn't get the same support, the same outcry.' While the prime minister, mayor of London and home secretary all went on record to express their sympathy with Sarah's family and friends, Ms Smallman received no such response from senior politicians. In the 'pecking order of things', she said, black women 'are the lowest on the ladder'.

Then there are the deaths of migrant women, who are often forced to choose between homelessness or returning to their abusers because of a hostile environment policy that leaves them with no recourse to public funds. The deaths of older women, like Julia James, a 53-year-old police community support officer who was murdered exactly three months after Sarah Everard, apparently do not provoke the same outpouring of public emotion, nor do they warrant the same number of column inches. The man who slit his disabled wife's throat as she slept, yet was sympathetically described as a 'jilted husband' in headlines about the murder. Or the deaths of 278 women aged sixty and over who were killed by men between 2009 and 2018: the men often receiving shockingly lenient sentences; the women being discussed in the context of 'hen-pecking', nagging stereotypes. In a 2020 poll of the public by charity Hourglass, over a fifth didn't view pushing, hitting or beating an older person as abuse.

This is not to say that the outcry over Sarah Everard's

death was not warranted or right and not to undermine for one moment the unconscionable tragedy of her murder or the devastating impact it will have had on all those who knew her, as well as so many who did not. It is only to say that there are others, too. Other dead women, killed by men, whose stories go untold. Whose names we never hear. Whose pieces of the jigsaw we are not able to see.

Andrea Simon, director of the End Violence Against Women Coalition, says:

> The particular spotlight on violence against women and girls that occurred after the tragic murder of Sarah Everard propelled a national conversation about women's safety and the need to reassure women they were safe in public spaces, but it also sparked other conversations about which women are routinely invisible within our media and public narratives because of race, age and other characteristics.
>
> The idea of a perfect, blameless victim relies on harmful sexist and also racist myths and stereotypes. Women and girls who are black or minority ethnic, disabled, LGBTQ or who face multiple disadvantages too often encounter institutional discrimination in their interactions with criminal justice agencies, which becomes a barrier to accessing justice.
>
> Black women are invisible in the justice system because the CPS [Crown Prosecution Service] doesn't produce disaggregated stats on prosecutorial outcomes, even though women who are black or mixed race are disproportionately likely to be victims of rape according to ONS data. It is not good enough to expect justice outcomes to improve for some women; we need to make progress on equality of access to justice and far better outcomes for all survivors of violence.

When Sarah died, people sat up and took notice. Her photograph was on the front page of every major newspaper. And the police needed to remind us that this was incredibly rare. That this was an *isolated incident*. Because nobody wants us to join the dots and realise that it doesn't matter what we do. Women are dying everywhere. One every three days. And we are not the problem. It isn't because we fucked up or wore the wrong thing or went the wrong way. It is because men are killing us. But we don't talk about the men. We focus on the women. So the women needed to be reminded that this was: Just. An. Isolated. Incident.

Metropolitan Police Commissioner Cressida Dick gave a statement. 'It is thankfully incredibly rare for a woman to be abducted from our streets,' she said. 'But I completely understand that, despite this, women in London and the wider public – particularly those in the area where Sarah went missing – will be worried and may well be feeling scared.'

Unlike the thousands of women who had been sharing their own experiences on social media, their own near-misses and terrifying memories of being followed home by men and assaulted in public spaces, Dick did not place the events in the broader context of a world in which women know that they are unsafe on a daily basis – not just in and around an area where one attack has been committed, but everywhere. She didn't recognise that this was part of a spectrum of behaviours, from the abduction and murder of a woman down to the fact that over 70 per cent of all women and 86 per cent of young woman have been sexually harassed in public in the UK.

The mainstream media followed suit. On 11 March, the front page of *The Times* read: 'Police insist women safe as remains discovered.' BBC Radio 4's *Today* programme, one of our biggest flagship media outlets, invited on the criminologist Marian

FitzGerald to emphasise that men were at a greater risk of experiencing violence than women. 'I think I'm entitled to say, as a woman, we shouldn't pander to stereotypes and get hysterical. Let's not get this out of proportion,' she told Nick Robinson. A producer at the programme must have made the choice to invite her on, after a researcher had sounded her out, knowing that this was the perspective they were choosing to platform that day, the 'spin' they wanted to put on the story. It matters. It shapes our national narrative. It adds fuel to the fire of the dismissals and the cries of 'not all men' and 'what about the men'.

And yes, of course, men experience violence, too. Yes, that's a valid problem to discuss (though raising it in this context, as so many did, was a clear and deliberate attempt to move the focus away from violence against women). But there was a glaring elephant in the room – one nobody ever seems to think it relevant to mention. Those men are victims of male violence, too. Yes, if we frame this with the victims as the central focus, then violence against women and violence against men seem like different, separate problems. But, if we frame this correctly, if we are brave enough to name the problem, though we still find it so very uncomfortable and difficult to do so, then we can see that we are really taking about the same thing: *male violence.*

But we don't do that. We talk about the women. Women who have been raped. Numbers of women murdered or sexually harassed. We don't talk about the men harassing or raping or murdering them. Even though that is what's happening. Even when to do so requires a deliberate blindness that borders on the absurd.

'Family tribute to woman found on fire in street,' read a BBC News headline in August 2021 after Sarah Hussein died in Bury. 'Devastated family of woman who died after being found on fire "miss her every day",' read another headline. Three men were arrested on suspicion of her murder, but, to read the headlines, you would think she had spontaneously combusted. Women do not spontaneously combust.

So they told us to stop making a fuss. To see this as a one-off. Not just the police and the media, but the politicians, too. When female MPs raised the issue in parliament, asking for stronger measures against sexual violence, they were scolded for getting over-emotional.

In the wake of protests across the UK about racism and colonialism, some of which focused on statues that commemorate and celebrate men whose legacies often rest on racist violence and subjugation, the Police, Crime Sentencing and Courts Bill sought to introduce protections for statues. Questioning the unacknowledged impact and lingering influence of such shrines to a colonial, deeply harmful past in our modern society was apparently beyond the pale. Action must be taken – and urgently – to protect these blocks of stone. Real, living and breathing women? Not so much. But to remark upon this was apparently an overreaction. An emotional, embarrassing outburst worthy of disapproving censure.

Shadow Culture Secretary Jo Stevens asked Culture Secretary Oliver Dowden about the bill in parliament, pointing out that it 'provides for longer sentences for hitting statues than those that have been given for raping women'. Dowden replied, 'I really wish that Members in this House would take a more temperate approach towards this.' But the temperate approach, it seemed, was only required for women talking about rape. In the same breath, Dowden went on to speak about the 'tremendous emotional value' of statues and, in his very next answer, he congratulated a male colleague for his 'passionate concern' about tourism. Some things are worthy of political passion, then, but rape is not one of them.

In a debate about domestic abuse and rape that same morning, the attorney general told a female Labour MP, 'I don't think the emotive language the Honourable Lady uses is appropriate at all.' The MP in question, Ellie Reeves, had asked about the 'effective decriminalisation of rape' in the UK. The response made it sound like another 'hysterical' overreaction. Except that Reeves was speaking literally. Not emotively. Just stating the facts. Because, in the UK now, even in the rare situation when a rape case is reported to police, there is just a 1.4 per cent chance it will result in a charge or summons for the perpetrator. Not even a conviction. Just a charge or a summons. When someone has a 99 per cent chance of getting away with a crime with zero legal repercussions, isn't it quite reasonable to refer to it as having been effectively decriminalised?

Protest

Calling women hysterical isn't accurate or warranted. But it *is* a useful way to try to shame women into shutting up while, at the same time, scoffing at them and undermining their point. Both of which would have been useful to politicians and police in the wake of Sarah's disappearance. It would have been useful if women had just shut up and stopped making a fuss. Stopped trying to make the point that there was a bigger problem here than just a single case. A crisis that demanded a huge and joined-up approach to tackle it effectively.

But women didn't shut up. They wanted to grieve, so they organised a vigil. A peaceful gathering to mourn Sarah. But they were told it was too risky, too dangerous during COVID-19. Never mind that numerous large-scale protests had taken place in London throughout the pandemic, including several anti-lockdown and anti-vaccination marches. Never mind that this was a vigil, not a protest; a gathering of hundreds, not thousands, to mourn a woman's life cut short. And, in a country in which one woman falls to male violence every three days, it was galling that the police, the same police who had failed to protect Sarah and who fail to protect so many other women, told the mourners to think of 'safety' and to 'find a safe alternative way to express their views'. Telling us to stay safe! Really? Did nobody who read those press releases appreciate the bitter irony?

Of course, this highlighted the exact moment at which the police and others begin to care about women's safety: when it threatens to impact other people as well. Much in the same way that, when the perpetrators of domestic abuse, sexual harassment and assault perpetrate acts of mass violence, law enforcement suddenly takes notice of them. Because suddenly the victims are not 'just' women.

And, when the usual attempts to pacify and silence us didn't work, the state resorted to violence instead.

Police didn't seem particularly concerned about women's well-being as they moved in at the event, where a few hundred women had gathered in defiance of the threat of legal action, and began to wrestle grieving participants to the ground and drag them away. Strangely, similar scenes did not play out in subsequent months when thousands of mostly male football fans gathered in enormous crowds in public spaces, often in defiance of COVID-19 social distancing regulations, to watch the Euros, a tournament linked to 2,000 cases of COVID-19 in Scotland alone.

But an inquiry took place and a report was written by a police watchdog. It was found that the police had 'acted appropriately' on the night of the vigil and that officers 'did their best'. Which is reassuring, isn't it? We are lucky that such impartial processes exist to help us make sure that nothing untoward or misogynistic is happening within the institutions that govern our public lives. Oh, did I mention that over half of those on the panel were former police officers themselves?

Spoiled barrel

Rightly, Sarah Everard's case threw a spotlight on police actions in relation to violence against women. Not only because of the woefully poor police response in the aftermath of the tragedy, but also because the man arrested and charged with Sarah's rape and murder was a police officer himself.

A police officer. After police officers told us to keep ourselves safe. After police officers dragged women away by their hair when they tried to grieve. After people told us to 'just go to the police', as though the women who don't report sexual violence or harassment are to blame if justice isn't done. As though the police force itself isn't institutionally suffused with the same sexism, racism and prejudice that prevents women from speaking out in society more widely, that enables and normalises their abuse in the first place and that forces them to carry it silently on their own shoulders.

Dame Cressida Dick was quick to respond to the dots people were joining. On the day that PC Wayne Couzens, forty-eight, pleaded guilty to the kidnapping and rape of Sarah Everard, Dick gave a speech in which she said that there was an 'occasion[al] bad 'un' in the Metropolitan Police. In dealing with such officers, Dick claimed, 'We are intolerant and we set ourselves high standards in how we work to identify and tackle and prevent any such behaviours.'

This was very reassuring. It is impossible, you might argue, to prevent the misogyny already existing so widely within our society from infiltrating the police force to some degree, but how reassuring to know that, if signs of it are shown, it will not be tolerated. It will be identified and tackled and prevented.

Except . . .

Except that Wayne Couzens was reported to the Metropolitan Police (yes, the same police force he worked for) for indecent exposure after allegedly exposing his genitals to a woman working in a south London takeaway restaurant just three days before Sarah Everard disappeared. And the response from this police force, with its 'high standards' and its intolerance, was so ineffective that Couzens was still on duty, still working as a serving officer in the job that brought him to London three days later where he targeted Sarah after the end of his shift.

Just a mistake, perhaps? A delay in the process? A misunderstanding? That a man should expose his genitals to a woman in her place of work and be left free to continue discharging his duty as a police officer in subsequent days – maybe it was just a blip?

Except . . .

It soon emerged that this wasn't the first time Couzens had been reported to the police for indecent exposure while he was serving as a police officer. Dating as far back as 2015, Couzens had, in fact, been investigated over three separate incidents, all of them under investigation by the Independent Office for Police Conduct (IOPC) at the time of writing. Let's hope those investigations are as thorough as the one that cleared all the officers of wrongdoing on the night of Everard's vigil.

Of course, the fact that Couzens had repeatedly been reported for exposing himself indecently and had repeatedly been allowed to continue as a police officer doesn't disprove Dick's claim about occasional bad apples, though it makes her insistence that such bad apples are staunchly routed out fairly difficult to swallow. Perhaps Couzens was just one of those 'occasional' bad 'uns, except there was more. By July that year, the IOPC admitted that twelve Metropolitan Police officers were under investigation in relation to Sarah's case. Not one or two potential 'bad 'uns'. Twelve. Not twelve across all the thousands of cases the Met was handling at the time. Just on this one case.

One of the officers being investigated, a Met Police constable, was alleged to have shared with other officers an 'inappropriate graphic relating to the case' over social media, before taking up his post manning the cordon at the scene of the search for Sarah. Just a joke. Don't get your knickers in a twist. Lighten up, love.

What difference does a joke make? She was already dead. But she might not have died if more 'minor' instances of abuse against women by men had been taken seriously by members of that force. If they'd seen it as a significant enough transgression to respond to a report of indecent exposure immediately and learned that the perpetrator was a serving police officer. If our society didn't see flashing a woman as a bit of a joke. This was the same force whose officers were joking about Sarah while they were supposed to be tasked with finding her. Who allegedly shared 'jokes' on WhatsApp about luring a woman into the woods and killing her, even as the search continued. The same force, in fact, that was already under investigation after two officers had taken photographs of the crime scene and dead bodies of Bibaa Henry and Nicole Smallman – photographs, it would later emerge, that had been shared with sick sexist commentary in a WhatsApp group called 'A Team' that included forty-one Metropolitan Police officers. The same force in which, it would also emerge, two officers had been in a separate WhatsApp group with Couzens and two officers from other forces, sharing misogynistic, racist and homophobic messages for over two years. Did I mention that Wayne Couzens' own colleagues at the Civil Nuclear Constabulary openly nicknamed him 'The Rapist' because he made women feel so uncomfortable? That he had this reputation among his peers before he passed the supposedly stringent vetting procedures to become a Metropolitan Police officer? The notion of a single bad apple becomes absurd. It was ironic, really, that Dick chose that particular metaphor. Did she forget the rest of the saying? One bad apple . . . spoils the whole barrel.

The night that women gathered to mourn Sarah's death and police officers dragged them away, a woman was walking home from the vigil when a man exposed himself on the street in front of her. The same offence Wayne Couzens had twice been accused of without any serious action being taken before he raped and murdered Sarah. The woman told the BBC that she approached a group of police officers to report what had happened and asked them to intervene. 'We're not dealing with it,' the woman said the police told her.

This is where the outright refusal to acknowledge institutional misogyny in the police force meets the normalisation of that misogyny within our society. Where the police refusal to take indecent exposure seriously meshes with our societal 'jokes' about so-called 'peeping Toms' and 'dirty old men' in raincoats. Where we transform the perpetrator of a sexual violation into a harmless, funny figure of sympathy or ridicule, with that attitude influencing the way in which those perpetrators are treated by the justice system. Where we fail, yet again, to join the dots between the low-level 'banter' and 'compliments' women endure daily and their rapes and deaths.

Couzens was far from the first 'flasher' to progress to more serious crimes. Pawel Relowicz, the man convicted of raping and murdering student Libby Squire in 2019, had targeted numerous other women in the lead-up to Libby's disappearance, including watching female students through windows, leaving used condoms and underwear at the scenes of his voyeurism, and masturbating in front of women in the street. If those offences had been taken seriously enough, might he have been stopped before Libby died?

The student victim of one of Relowicz's acts of voyeurism told the BBC that people made her feel like she was 'blowing it out of proportion' when she reported an incident in which he had watched her being intimate with her boyfriend through a window, leaving a used condom and women's underwear on the front doorstep afterwards. 'I think they just thought it was funny, but I didn't find it funny at all,' she said. It was only after her mother, a former police officer, 'nudged them' that the police arrived – a day later – to take fingerprints. (The force told the BBC that 'a proportionate investigation with the information available at the time' had taken place and that it had treated the victim's report 'with the appropriate level of seriousness'.)

When the details of Relowicz's history came to light in 2021, even after it was known that he had murdered Libby, dozens of news headlines used the term 'peeping Tom' to describe him.

The Everyday Sexism Project is littered with thousands of entries relating to indecent exposure. They are full of phrases like: 'Nobody seemed bothered'; 'They said we were making it up'; 'Everyone laughed'; and 'I never dreamed of reporting it'.

Despite Libby Squire, despite so many other women like her, fewer than a tenth of the 113,000 women who experience indecent exposure each year (according to the ONS) report it to the police. And little wonder: of almost 11,000 cases of 'exposure and voyeurism' reported to police in the year to March 2020, just 594 suspects were taken to court.

A huge part of this comes back to the fact that we simply don't take the traumatic sexual violation of women seriously when it happens in the form of indecent exposure, voyeurism, unwanted 'dick pics', wolf whistles and catcalls. We think it is funny. We ridicule those who feel impacted by it.

> Ten years ago, I was masturbated on in my university library; I was listening to music and didn't see him behind me until too late. Told my friends and everyone (male and female) thought it was hilarious. The police never followed it up, neither did the university, and I didn't pursue it because I felt like I was making a fuss. It's only now I realise how upsetting the incident was.

But all these behaviours are on a spectrum. All are about men exerting sexual power and control over women and often getting off on the fact that they know women are helpless to protest and won't be taken seriously if they do. Often, they lead to more and more serious offending until, in some cases, a woman dies.

This is where the societal attitude system that sees us dismiss and ignore women and convince them that they're crazy, overreacting or must have 'asked for it' meets the institutional systems that fail victims and survivors – the point at which those ideas about women harden and crystallise into ingrained misogyny and insurmountable barriers to justice.

ROTTEN APPLES

As it turns out, it wasn't just the twelve potential 'bad 'uns'. Almost 600 sexual misconduct allegations were made against Metropolitan Police officers between 2012 and 2018, but only 119 of those were upheld, including one officer who was sacked after having sex with a rape victim and one who assaulted a domestic abuse survivor. At the time of writing, a West Mercia Police officer is on bail, accused of rape and five counts of sexual assault against two women. Elsewhere, a probationary officer at West Midlands Police, who verbally abused a woman, grabbing her by the neck and forcing her to the floor, was not jailed, but simply given a curfew. And an officer from West Yorkshire Police will go on trial this year, accused of raping and sexually assaulting a woman. Meanwhile, the Met is currently investigating allegations that a serving officer raped two female colleagues. Three years after the allegations were first made, he has not been suspended.

I was out for a drink with colleagues on Friday and was the only female in the group. At one point, two of them decided to ask me: if I had to be raped by one of them, which one would I prefer. Seeing the look of disbelief on my face, they then rephrased the question to ask: if they were both rapists, which one would I not mind. I was absolutely horrified and asked them if they were serious. Several of my other male colleagues looked uncomfortable, but didn't say anything. I made my excuses and left with a smile on my face, but inwardly furious. I'm in my late forties and these colleagues were a few years older. We're all police officers.

In August 2021, a former police officer pleaded guilty to sexually exploiting two domestic abuse victims after using his position to groom them while on duty. It had taken almost two decades for the women to report the incident as they'd felt 'too intimidated to speak out due to his position as a police officer', said the official CPS report, also quietly dropping in the fact that one of the women had actually made a complaint of indecent assault when the officer had forcibly kissed her, though it did not explain why the officer had then continued to serve.

In 2021, six officers from Hampshire Constabulary's Serious Organised Crime Unit were found guilty of gross misconduct after a covert bug recorded them in the workplace referring to women directly and indirectly as 'whores', 'sluts', 'sweet tits', 'sugar tits' and 'fucking Dorises', as well as pondering among themselves whether the woman speaking over the Tannoy system was 'getting any cock'. Additionally, a woman who reported domestic abuse to the police later received a voicemail accidentally left by the officers who were supposed to be investigating the incident. They had inadvertently recorded themselves referring to her as a 'bitch' and a 'fucking slag'.

I was appalled by the way rape victims were spoken about. I had only been in the job six months when my crewmate showed around the evidence from a rape victim who had been left with very dirty underwear. The offending item was in a sealed forensic bag waiting to be booked into property when he ran about the office waving the stained crotch, visible through the clear seams of the bag, in people's faces. Oh, how they all laughed.

In 2022, the IOPC released a report into a group of investigations into discrimination, misogyny, harassment and bullying involving officers predominantly based at Charing Cross Police Station. The investigations revealed that misogyny, racism and homophobia were rife, with an 'underlying culture' and excuses of 'banter' allowing them to go unchallenged. In one WhatsApp group, an officer wrote: 'You ever slapped your missus? It makes them love you more . . . Now I know why these daft cunts are getting murdered by their spastic boyfriends. Knock a bird about and she will love you. Human nature. They are biologically programmed to like that shit.' Another message read: 'Getting a woman in to bed is like spreading butter. It can be done with a bit of effort using a credit card, but it's quicker and easier just to use a knife.' Male officers sent messages to their female colleagues saying things like: 'I would happily rape you.' These are just some of the cases that have hit the headlines in the past year alone. These men are part of a system, the same system that routinely fails to take women seriously and utterly fails to deliver them justice. The IOPC report into the officers in Charing Cross explicitly said: 'We believe these incidents are not isolated or simply the behaviour of a few 'bad apples'.' Yet in spite of the overwhelming evidence in the report and elsewhere, an official Met response claimed: 'We do not believe there is a culture of misogyny in the Met.' Most damning of all, 9 of the 14 officers investigated are still serving in the force.

Data gathered by the Centre for Women's Justice in 2020 found a total of 666 reports of domestic abuse-related incidents and offences perpetrated by police officers, police community support officers and other staff during a three-year period. One survivor described how her partner would threaten to have her arrested if she reported him. Another spoke of her ex-partner and abuser telling her, 'I'm a police officer, no one's going to believe you.' The report concluded: 'We are concerned that the types of conduct discussed in this super-complaint arise from a wider culture within the police service that condones and trivialises violence against women, an "institutionalised sexism".'

The report was right. These are not isolated incidents. A 2016 survey of over 1,700 police staff members across England, Scotland and Wales found that 49 per cent of the staff had experienced the repeated telling of sexualised jokes, almost a fifth had received sexually explicit emails or texts and almost a fifth had been touched at work in a way that made them feel uncomfortable. Almost one in ten had been told that sexual favours could lead to preferential treatment.

I am the only female on a section of emergency response police officers. I am the butt of daily jokes, none of which are funny, all of which are tedious. I am called 'slit arse', 'whoopsy' and told frequently to get in the kitchen and make the tea – because that's all we are good for apparently . . . The men I have to endure working with look at porn on their mobiles almost daily and make revolting and shallow comments about my female colleagues and female members of the public. If a female officer gets promoted to a specialist role, I have to endure days of their bitter remarks about positive discrimination. I have never heard any of them praise a female officer for her achievements on merit.

We have to look at these systemic issues within policing in the context of the way in which police are handling sexual violence crimes. Not only the fact that just 1.4 per cent of reported rape cases result in a charge or summons, but also the fact that three in four domestic abuse cases close without charge in England and Wales. Three-quarters. Even after a victim has finally plucked up the courage to report to the police in the first place (which, evidence tells us, can take years: on average, victims endure fifty incidents of abuse before getting help), they are often failed at the last hurdle. Evidence suggests that reporting to the police very rarely fixes the problem swiftly and effectively. In fact, on average, domestic abuse survivors report to police 2.8 times before getting help. And yes, of course, there are challenges to policing these crimes, but these should not account for such an outrageously low charging rate. And, if such challenges were the only barrier to justice, we would expect to see very similar charging rates across the country. Instead, evidence reveals a postcode lottery: there are ten police forces in England and Wales in which 80 per cent of domestic abuse allegations are closed without charge, strongly suggesting that the issue is with the police force itself, not the nature of the crime.

In the week Wayne Couzens was sentenced, the Metropolitan Police released a statement that they'd had months to prepare and consider. It contained guidance for women who might feel unsafe if they were stopped by a lone police officer in the wake of Couzens' offences. The advice offered was this: 'Wave down a bus.' No, really. That's *actually* what they suggested. After months of presumably quite careful consideration, that is what they came up with. Someone who didn't feel safe or able to verify a police officer's credentials could consider 'shouting out to a passer-by, running into a house, knocking on a door, waving a bus down or, if you are in the position to do so, calling 999', the statement said.

So determined seemed the police not to acknowledge institutional misogyny that they also released a litany of ways in which women could check the credentials of officers who stopped them. For instance: ringing up a police control room to check an officer's identification number. Which I'm sure Wayne Couzens would have patiently waited for Sarah Everard to do, had she asked. One helpful police force tweeted a photo of a genuine officer's warrant card, alongside a fake one, which was probably well-meaning, but who carries a magnifying glass and a torch on a night out to scrutinise a police ID for signs of imitation? More importantly, the advice completely missed the point: Couzens had a genuine warrant card because he was a real police officer. The problem here was not men dressing up as police officers to abduct women. It was a police force with a rapist and murderer ensconced within its ranks.

Besides which, what kind of response do we expect to get from officers when we try to verify their credentials and question their motives in arresting us? A question particularly pertinent, as many people pointed out, for black and minoritised women, already part of a community disproportionately targeted by police and more likely to experience hostile and violent police responses. Were those women in the Met's minds when they were telling people to run from the arresting officer and attempt to hail a bus? Or disabled women, for some of whom 'just' running away would not be an option? It's almost like they didn't bother to think it through. But that couldn't be the case. Not after they had assured us so many times that women's safety was a priority. Not when they had had months to prepare this response to Couzens' awful crimes.

Following a new wave of drink-spiking offences in 2021, the BBC interviewed a sergeant from Devon and Cornwall Police, the force which leads on tackling drink-spiking across the country. The sergeant, who had reportedly 'been working on prevention methods for years', had this to say: he would like to see individuals carry drink-testing kits with them on nights out. 'It just makes you more of a harder target . . . It could be one of those things people take to clubs or house parties, very much like having condoms.'

Except that you take condoms with you in case you have consensual sex. Telling women (and let's not pretend this wasn't really aimed largely at women) to carry an entire drink-testing kit with them on a night out is like telling them to expect and accept that their drink being spiked might just be a routine part of the evening. Like saying, 'Take an umbrella, love, it looks like rain.' So how many times during the evening should I test my drink? Before each sip? Or do I have to chug the whole thing in one go once tested, so as to avoid giving anyone a second chance? And this is apparently coming from the leading force in the whole country on this issue. Not proposing tougher sanctions. Not proposing searches for men entering clubs. Just adding yet another ridiculous job for women to undertake as part of their 'fun' night out.

Pick up your magnifying glass and shoulder your drink-testing kit. Strap on your anti-rape underwear. Make sure to remember your attack alarm, your pepper spray, your adorable pink ring that doubles as a small self-protection weapon. Better still, take a pack of highly trained dogs on short leashes and some kind of small explosive device capable of neutralising potential assailants. But, hang on, isn't all that gear going to slow you down when you're trying to run into the path of the nearest bus? You know what? To be on the safe side, just stay at home or, come to think of it, check yourself into the nearest police station and ask them to lock you in a cell for maximum security. Oh no, wait. You can't be sure you'll be safe there either, can you? What if one of Wayne Couzens' WhatsApp mates happens to be on duty?

We know that the vast majority of victims of sexual violence and domestic abuse simply never feel able to report to the police at all, in part because of the huge barriers to justice they know they will face, the fear of being mocked, disbelieved or blamed for what happened, or simply the sense that it will not be taken seriously. The black women who find that stereotypes and assumptions prevent police officers from taking their reports seriously. The black women who struggle to overcome the 'strong black woman' trope in a society whose collective concept of the archetypal fragile, young, white, virginal victim has been shaped by racist and colonial history. The black women whose bruises may be ignored because they appear differently from injuries on white skin.

Women like Valerie Forde, who reported her partner's threats to police six weeks before he brutally murdered her and her 23-month-old daughter. Police had recorded her report as a threat to property rather than a threat to life.

Or the sex worker who was assaulted at work. When she tried to report it, she was told that, 'by nature of her occupation, consent had been implied'.

You can see the impact of such assumptions time after time in the hundreds of stories women have shared with the Everyday Sexism Project after trying to report sexual violence.

> I was asked questions such as 'what was I wearing', 'do my friends consider me promiscuous', 'had I had sex before', 'do I have a

boyfriend', 'how many times have I had sex' and more and more. It was honestly humiliating. And I had to do everything to hold back the tears. The justice system needs to change.

New Year's Eve. Central London crowd. I was grabbed in the crotch by a man who looked me in the eyes while he did it. I reported it almost immediately to two police officers not 5 metres away. I was sobbing. One looked at the other and shrugged, 'She's drunk.'

I was physically attacked by a man when I was about twenty-five. The police asked me if I had been wearing the vest top I had on at the time (height of summer and very hot) and if the marks on my neck, where he attempted to strangle me, were 'love bites'.

The police [told me] that I hadn't been assaulted, that because I had kissed this guy earlier I had consented to all sexual acts that followed.

Is it any surprise that just 15 per cent of those who experience sexual violence feel able to report it to the police?

It's not just how the police treat the women themselves that matters. It's what they do with their cases, too. A shocking report in 2014 revealed that over a quarter of all sexual offences reported to the police are not even recorded as crimes. An investigation found that a fifth of the decisions to 'no-crime' rape reports were incorrect. (A 'no-crime' occurs when a recorded crime is later cancelled because supposedly verifiable information shows that a crime was not actually committed.) The report found that the rate of no-criming for rape cases was more than double the average rate for all crime recorded by police. Examples of victim-blaming and rape myths abounded in the report: in one case of a 'no-crime', officers simply didn't believe a thirteen-year-old girl's account of rape because there were no witnesses or evidence. In another example, the case was no-crimed 'on the basis that, because she had taken some of her clothes off, she must be presumed to have consented to sexual intercourse, despite her insistence that she did not'.

A woman who has experienced a rape knows that, if she can stomach the traumatic experience of recounting it to the police, whether or not she actually gets a shot at justice then depends on the decision of an individual in a heavily male-dominated, systemically misogynistic institution.

> I've talked to the police about it; the male officer told me it would be one word against another and that, if I reported it, it might aggravate him further . . . So what do I do? Forget about it? Let him go on to threaten to rape or actually rape someone else? I feel I have wasted my time reporting it. . . . The police don't want to know.

None of this is new – from attacks by Jack the Ripper to the Yorkshire Ripper, we have seen the lack of justice afforded to victims of male violence when the people charged with investigating their assaults and murders make stereotyped, misogynistic assumptions about the victims. We saw it in Rotherham, where some 1,400 children were sexually abused over a period of sixteen years, with authorities failing to act on information about widespread sexual exploitation, in part because vulnerable, underage girls – many of them in care and from poor socio-economic backgrounds – were seen by police as being complicit in their own abuse. 'We were [seen as] "slags" and "little criminals",' one survivor later said.

It is always about the women. Never about the system.

This is not to suggest that every police officer is racist or misogynistic or that there aren't brilliant, hard-working members of the police force doing everything in their power to fight violence against women. But it is a clear and ridiculous act of denial to suggest, in light of these statistics, that we are just talking about a few bad apples. It is clear that this is an institutional issue and one that cannot be solved by sticking heads in the sand and talking about a few anomalous 'bad 'uns'.

Describing a form of inequality as institutionalised does not mean accusing every individual involved in that institution of being prejudiced. It means recognising that the problem is sufficiently pervasive and unaddressed within an institution that it goes further than just isolated incidents, resulting in it impacting on the culture and output of the institution.

We might, for example, consider the following conditions as a good indicator of whether or not institutional sexism exists:

- Is there a significant gender gap within the institution (e.g. in staffing, senior leadership or pay)?
- Are there a large number of incidents of sexism, sexual harassment or assault occurring within the institution?
- Does the institution fail to demonstrate robust policies, consistently applied, to prevent and respond to such issues?
- Is there evidence that the actions and output of the institution have a harmful impact on women?

In the case of policing, we could answer each of these questions with a resounding yes. Police forces are significantly male-dominated. Men still make up at least two-thirds of officers across all ranks in England and Wales and, in the biggest force, the Metropolitan Police, men outnumber women 2.5 to 1.

A worryingly high number of allegations of sexual violence and domestic abuse have been made against police officers, particularly in the context of vetting procedures supposedly designed to result in a much lower number of such incidents. We have seen copious recent evidence that these policies are insufficient (as evidenced by the many missed opportunities to stop Wayne Couzens). And, perhaps most worryingly of all, in the same week Couzens was sentenced, almost a third of police forces in England and Wales referred allegations of sexual assault and harassment against their own officers to the police watchdog. These twenty-seven referrals from fourteen forces, described by the watchdog as a 'significant increase' from previous weeks, strongly suggest that the police had not been taking the problem as seriously as they should have before it hit the national spotlight. Either they didn't have procedures in place to tackle reported incidents or they simply hadn't been following them until that moment. To put it more clearly still, we know from freedom-of-information requests that just one in eighteen members of the Metropolitan Police accused of sexual assault is ever subject to formal action against them.

The external impact of all this is overwhelmingly obvious – the alarming rate of wrongly 'no-crimed' rapes, the women whose experiences of reporting to the police reveal devastating victim-blaming, the appallingly low numbers of cases leading to a charge or summons. Women are not blissfully unaware of the misogyny running through our police forces. We've all heard the stories, seen the coverage. Everyone knows someone who has had a bad experience. Institutional sexism is a major deterrent to reporting in the first place, let alone encountering it first-hand, which increases the rate of attrition even when cases do get reported. A study into rape and justice in Ireland found that over 40 per cent of those survivors who had reported their rape to the Gardaí seriously considered withdrawing their complaint – the primary reason for this was a poor reaction from the Gardaí.

When all these factors are combined, we have a very strong argument for describing policing as institutionally sexist.

And, if there were any remaining doubt, it is hard not to consider that shattered by the words of Police Commissioner Philip Allott, who was interviewed on the radio in the wake of Sarah Everard's murder. This was the man responsible for overseeing all of North Yorkshire Police; a major cog in the policing machine. He said: 'Women, first of all, need to be streetwise about when they can be arrested and when they can't be arrested. She should never have been arrested and submitted to that.' Allott later resigned, but only after a sustained and powerful public backlash to his words. Like the punishment of the officers who took photos of Bibaa Henry and Nicole Smallman, who were dismissed and jailed, this cannot be seen as progress in and of itself. It is only the system protecting itself when it is, very occasionally, exposed. But Allott had been a council leader and a mayor. He had, for years, been a powerful part of the system and would have continued to be for years to come had he not happened to be interviewed on the radio that day.

'She never should have submitted.' As though it were her fault. As though it would have made any difference if she had tried to refuse. As though women are not socialised our whole lives to be submissive and pliant and non-confrontational. As though we shouldn't have every reason to trust a police officer.

But perhaps, in a twisted way, Allott was right. We should not submit. We should not trust. We should recognise that the system is rotten.

PUTTING THE VICTIM ON TRIAL

Policing is not the only broken institution. In the past few years, we have witnessed a shocking collapse in the volume and percentage of rape allegations resulting in a prosecution. Since 2016–17, rape prosecutions have plummeted to an unprecedented low: in 2020–21, there were just 1,557 prosecutions in England and Wales, despite over 55,000 cases being reported to police. Charges in rape cases are now exactly half what they were in 2015–16, representing an alarmingly rapid decline. In a landmark report on 'the decriminalisation of rape', leading women's charities set out a powerful argument that rape cases were being dropped when they shouldn't be. The report included a devastating dossier of rape cases the CPS had decided not to charge, including a woman held at knifepoint, a woman whose rape was filmed, with footage found on the suspect's phone, and a case for which the CPS's reason not to bring charges was that the survivor 'enjoyed an adventurous sex life'.

What was most concerning was the allegation in the report that CPS guidance and training had shifted dramatically in recent years, with prosecutors encouraged to remove 'weak' rape cases that might be 'less likely to find favour with a jury'. 'If we took 350 weak cases out of the system, our conviction rate goes up to 61 per cent,' as one whistle-blower said they were instructed in a training session.

The problem with this approach is that, once again, it aligns a system (in this case, our justice system) with the insidious ideas that are rampant in our society. Gender stereotypes, myths about sexual violence, notions of who is 'asking for it' and confusion about consent. Around the same time that whistle-blowers claimed the training shifted, guidance encouraging prosecutors to take a 'merits-based approach' to cases, instead of making charging decisions based on how a jury might respond, disappeared from the CPS website and training manuals. And the dates correspond directly with the significant decrease in the numbers of suspects charged, starting in 2017–18.

'Many colleagues have positively embraced the "bookmaker's approach" to charge,' noted a whistle-blower. 'They feel empowered to stop the prosecution of more "difficult" cases, which, based on their previous experience, have little prospect of resulting in a successful outcome at trial, such as so-called "student rape cases" involving alcohol.'

'Sexual offenders often target vulnerable victims, such as children, people with disabilities and people with chaotic lifestyles, because they know it is unlikely that they will be believed by a jury,' the whistle-blower's statement noted. If prosecutors are playing a guessing game about potential juror prejudices, those already-marginalised victims are likely to be worst affected.

But it's okay. Have you guessed why? That's right, there was a review. A judicial review brought by campaigners from the End Violence Against Women Coalition (EVAW), supported by the Centre for Women's Justice. And, without engaging in any meaningful way with the extensive evidence put forward by the EVAW, the judges (mostly men, of course) decided that the CPS had neither acted unlawfully nor irrationally and that, in fact, the changes in language and guidance for prosecutors did not constitute a change in policy or alter the way prosecutors approached rape cases. Even though it coincided with a catastrophic and unprecedented collapse in the volume and percentage of rape allegations resulting in a prosecution.

To support them in the legal case, the CPS brought in as a witness a chief crown prosecutor. She claimed that she did not think there had been any change in practice whatsoever in relation to rape-charging decisions in her area of the country in the period after prosecutors received training to stop applying the 'merits-based approach'. While this seemed to be taken at face value by the court, the reality is that data from the CPS itself showed that there had been a sudden charging-rate drop of over 60 per cent in her region specifically following the aforementioned training. But thank goodness for reviews. Thank goodness for reviews to keep things fair and make sure that these crimes, of which women comprise the vast majority of victims, are being fairly prosecuted. Thank goodness for reviews of our justice system carried out by our judiciary.

The same judiciary, by the way, in which fewer than a third of court judges are women – only 26 per cent of judges in the High Court and above, and 17 per cent of Queen's Counsel barristers. Meanwhile, just 8 per cent of court judges and 4 per cent of judges in the High Court and above are from black, Asian or minority ethnic backgrounds. And, in the Supreme Court, just two of the twelve justices are women. All are white.

If we take the same multi-pronged approach to considering whether an institution should be considered systemically sexist, then what is as worrying as the lack of diverse representation is the sort of judgement being handed down in cases relating to violence against women.

A man who sexually assaulted a terrified woman as she walked home alone at night avoided jail because he was the 'sole earner' in his family. 'If you feel a custodial sentence is required, he would lose his job and he is the sole earner for his family, so this would have a significant impact,' the perpetrator's lawyer told the court. Less consideration seems to have been given to the 'significant impact' felt by the victim, who, terrified of running into her attacker on the street, has since felt unable to leave her house or go to work. Would this defence have been so successful in a society less rigidly grounded in the gender stereotype of the male breadwinner? Would the court have been as likely to be convinced by the same argument if the perpetrator had been a woman?

Even the terminology we use to describe these offences shows how deeply gender stereotypes are embedded in our approach to justice. We see rape described as 'non-consensual sex'. But we would never refer to theft as 'non-consensual borrowing' or kidnap as a 'non-consensual excursion'. There is simply no other crime for which prejudices about the victim are so entrenched in the approach to investigation and prosecution. When someone is the victim of arson, nobody goes digging through their past to find out if they ever attended a bonfire party to imply that they might actually have secretly loved watching their house burn to the ground. Victims of burglary are not humiliatingly cross-examined in court about their previous habits of giving money to charity or accused of having 'flaunted' their wealth if they did so. And we do not confiscate the mobile phones of people who have experienced fraud to check if there is anything in their message history to suggest that they 'led the conman on'.

Anthony Williams strangled his wife, Ruth, to death three days into the first COVID-19 lockdown in Wales, fracturing her neck in five places and admitting to detectives that he had 'choked the living daylights' out of her. The court said that his mental state was 'severely affected at the time', after he told detectives he had found lockdown 'really hard' and his wife had suggested he 'get over it'. In other words – in the words of thousands of domestic abusers – he 'just snapped'. A psychiatrist said his anxiety and depressive illness were 'heightened' by the COVID measures, impairing his ability to exercise self-control. But another psychiatrist told the court that Williams had no documented history of suffering a depressive illness and therefore 'no psychiatric defences' available to him. Ultimately, he was convicted of manslaughter, not murder, and given a jail sentence of just five years.

Five years. For taking a woman's life. Because, after all, he had found lockdown so hard. This cannot be separated from a culture suffused with the idea of nagging wives and beleaguered husbands – from 'boys will be boys' and adverts about men tunnelling to freedom after being driven to desperate action by their awful spouses. It is all connected. Not directly, not simply. But subtly. In ways that are so hard to pin down or force people to see.

So surreal, so ridiculous is the situation we find ourselves in that one criminologist actually had to tell the media, 'To say that the lockdown is causing men to kill their wives is not accurate.' What have we come to that this actually needs to be spelled out?

And yes, it is gendered. It's always gendered. By comparison, a four-year study by the Centre for Women's Justice found that, when a woman 'just snaps' and kills her abuser after years of suffering domestic violence, she is almost as likely (43 per cent) to be convicted of murder as of manslaughter (46 per cent). Even if 'only' convicted of manslaughter, she is still likely to receive a sentence in the region of fourteen to eighteen years.

Harriet Wistrich, director of the Centre for Women's Justice, said: 'Yet again, we see deep-seated discriminatory attitudes laid bare by this latest sentencing, which, at its heart, rests on a culture of misogyny. It is clear that women who resist male violence are punished most severely, whereas men who throttle their wives to death for no apparent reason are just "tragic" figures.'

We can see the institutionalisation of societal sexism in sentences and judgements in which victim-blaming ideology is clearly at play. The man who walked free from court after being given just an eight-month suspended jail sentence, despite having admitted to 'engaging in sexual activity with a thirteen-year-old girl'. The judge and prosecution described his victim as sexually 'predatory', with the judge remarking during sentencing, 'I have taken into account that, even though the girl was thirteen, the prosecution say she looked and behaved a little bit older . . . On these facts, the girl was predatory and was egging you on.'

In 2017, an Idaho judge gave no prison time to a man who had raped a fourteen-year-old girl, instead blaming the rape on 'the social media system' and the 'sexual proclivities of young people'.

In a 2018 rape trial in Ireland, where a 27-year-old man was accused of raping a seventeen-year-old girl, the defence lawyer told the jury, 'You have to look at the way she was dressed. She was wearing a thong with a lace front.' The man was found not guilty of rape shortly afterwards.

We will blame almost anything, it seems, except the actual men who carry out these deliberate acts of violence.

And, like policing, the criminal justice system is by no means devoid of perpetrators of gendered violence – perpetrators who benefit from the same shocking sympathy, mitigation and excuses the system extends to others.

When a top court prosecutor from Worcester attempted to murder his wife in a frenzied knife attack as she lay in bed, he was jailed for just six years. The local newspaper covered the story like this: '[He] viciously attacked his wife after a bout of depression brought on by work pressures at the Crown Prosecution Service.'

Then there are the repeated lenient sentences for men who convince the court that, because a woman supposedly consented to 'rough sex', she somehow gave her consent to be choked to death. Daniel Lancaster, who claimed that his girlfriend 'enjoyed being throttled during intercourse', was found guilty of man-slaughter, not murder, and given just a four-year sentence. James Morton, twenty-four, strangled sixteen-year-old Hannah Pearson to death on the same day he met her and failed to call 999 for twenty minutes after she stopped breathing. His defence barrister argued that he had been 'pursuing his sexual thrill' and the jury cleared him of murder, instead giving him a twelve-year sentence for manslaughter.

It's like we just can't help ourselves. We cannot stop finding excuses for male violence. It starts with 'boys will be boys', it morphs into 'just a compliment', 'he couldn't help himself' and 'she was asking for it', and it ends up here.

Between 2009 and 2019, the use of the 'sex games gone wrong' defence rose by 90 per cent. When millionaire John Broadhurst killed his much younger partner, leaving her with forty injuries, serious internal trauma, a fractured eye socket and bleach on her face, he was given a sentence of three years, eight months for man-slaughter. He was freed after serving less than two years. This was despite the fact that her body had been found in a pool of blood at the bottom of the stairs; despite the fact that prosecutors said

Broadhurst had wanted to 'teach her a lesson' after finding out she'd been talking to ex-boyfriends; despite the fact that he didn't immediately phone an ambulance; despite the fact that, when paramedics eventually arrived, he told them she was 'dead as a doughnut'; despite the fact that he sprayed her face with bleach . . .

Despite all that, prosecutors chose to change the charge to manslaughter due to a 'realistic prospect of conviction'. Now, tell me again that women are not being systemically, outrageously failed by a criminal justice system that treats their lives as worthless and their deaths as minor infractions, depending on the likelihood of a misogynistic, victim-blaming jury to convict their rapists and murderers.

> When I was sixteen, I helped prosecute my father for years of physical and sexual abuse. His attorney made quite a few comments about how I'd wanted it. I was six when it started.

Justice is based in law, yes – but, when we think of that law as infallible and without prejudice, we forget two things. Firstly: that laws were mostly written by privileged white men. (I will never forget the day MP Caroline Lucas called me into her office and showed me with pride the first ever parliamentary bill not specific to a particular gender. Instead of just using male pronouns throughout, it included the words 'his or her'. Her staff had had to battle for this change, after being told, 'It just isn't done that way.') And secondly: that justice depends on the interpretation and application of law by police officers, prosecutors, juries and judges. And those groups of people are, as copious evidence reveals, by no means immune to racist, sexist and otherwise prejudiced beliefs and assumptions.

When we look at the ways in which the criminal justice system fails survivors of sexual violence, we are not just talking about the actions or biases of the people who work within that system. There are also structural issues that make prosecuting sexual violence particularly difficult. Our traditional, adversarial system of jury trials relies on presenting two different versions of events, incentivising defence advocates to approach rape cases by trying to destroy the credibility of the complainant.

The outcome rests on the opinion of twelve unvetted members of the public who are statistically highly likely to believe damaging rape myths like 'if she wasn't crying afterwards, she couldn't have been raped'. This is partly why decisions about whether or not to proceed to trial for rape, in comparison with other cases, can rely so damagingly on perceptions of whether or not a complainant will be expected to convince a jury – in other words, whether she fits the societal profile of the 'perfect victim'.

One woman's Everyday Sexism Project entry described her experience of jury duty on a sexual assault trial. She was dismayed when the 'cut and dried' case of assault was thrown out after the jury was unable to reach a unanimous conclusion because male jurors insisted that the girl should have shouted 'no' louder.

But these structural issues are not necessarily insurmountable. Women's charities have long suggested numerous potential solutions, such as: exploring the possibility of a more inquisitorial judicial approach in rape cases; reviewing courtroom cross-examination rules in rape cases; explicitly banning the use of sexual history evidence; and considering the possibility of judge-only or magistrate trials, rather than juries.

In the wake of a highly controversial rape trial in which two Ireland rugby players and their friends were acquitted of various charges (after the complainant was cross-examined for days on end by numerous male barristers, asked why she didn't scream, and had her bloodied underwear passed around by the jury), Fionnuala Ní Aoláin, Ireland's UN rapporteur on human rights, said, 'Law does violence to women, compounding the physical and emotional harms women experience from sexual harm. Masculinity pervades our courts.'

Everjoice Win is a Zimbabwean feminist activist who has spent decades working for gender equality through feminist and social justice movements in her home country, across the African continent and globally. Her work has shaped the women's human rights landscape in dozens of countries, including the passing of new laws and policies on domestic violence and inheritance, as well as shifting societal norms and values. In 2020, she was appointed professor of practice, women's rights, by SOAS, University of London. She says:

> There's a propensity very often in these cases for people to just turn to the law . . . 'The law must take its course,' you know? But we forget, again, that the law operates in the same society. The law is founded on these very same tenants, right? The attitudes, the mindsets of the judiciary, the people who are supposed to enforce this law . . . the police . . . are probably exactly the same, if not worse.

There is importance, she adds, in 'acknowledging how entrenched these things are'.

Normalisation breeds impunity

Let's look at another issue within our legal systems: the frequency of incidents of sexism and harassment and the ways in which they are dealt with.

In 2019, Lord Chief Justice Lord Burnett addressed the House of Lords after other leading lawyers had spoken out about sexism in the legal profession. Chris Henley QC had written an article about the misogyny faced by many of his female colleagues, describing the atmosphere at the Criminal Bar as 'increasingly hostile' and raising cases of women who had been 'treated monstrously'. Female barristers had chimed in, imploring their colleagues, among other requests, to stop making 'repetitive jokes about breasts or skirts. Don't communicate solely in innuendo.' Hardly an unreasonable ask, is it?

'I'm not aware of any evidence that women are deterred from applying to judicial office,' said the lord chief justice, perhaps the least likely person in the entire system to have been approached by any individual experiencing these problems. 'I fear', he went on, 'that there was a phenomenon in play that is all too familiar to politicians . . . The same examples [of sexism] get repeated time and time again and the impressions given are false . . . Of the hundreds of judges that sit in High Court and family court, if there is a problem that exists in this nature, it exists in a very small number.'

Of course, it is true that there are many brilliant judges who would not dream of acting in a prejudiced or discriminatory manner: many, indeed, who are making real, tangible efforts to create change within the system. Yet proof exists that this is not just, as the lord chief justice so dismissively suggested, the same handful of cases being recycled repeatedly. A 2020 study of over 700 solicitors, barristers and other women working in the legal profession showed that 58 per cent had experienced or witnessed sexism first-hand, but almost half did not complain for fear of the impact that doing so would have on their careers. In the same year, a black, female barrister was assumed to be a defendant three separate times in a single day when she was patronisingly told that 'only lawyers can go in' to the courtroom. And a senior government barrister, who was convicted of using his phone to film up a female passenger's skirt on the London Underground, was not struck off as a tribunal accepted that it was simply a 'heat of the moment' incident 'resulting from pressure at work' and the 'domestic pressures' arising from the fact that 'his wife was ill at the time'. Those poor men under pressure again.

> I did an advocacy course as a young lawyer. The retired judge teaching the course spoke about all the different styles of barrister (counsel): gifted orator, persuader, analytical and thorough. He was asked what challenges women faced as barristers. He said that being a woman was a style, too, as women counsel could 'flirt with the jury'.

It is difficult to equate all this with an unbiased, perfectly fair system. And, if we cannot trust those at the most senior levels of the legal system even to acknowledge misogyny within their own institution, let alone tackle it, how can they expect us to trust them to deliver any kind of justice to women experiencing crimes motivated by that same, apparently invisible misogyny?

The legal system not only fails women who have experienced rape or domestic abuse. In almost any situation in which women face harassment, discrimination or ill treatment on the basis of their gender, the obstacles to justice often seem insurmountable.

We've already seen just how rarely cases of indecent exposure ever reach court, and there's a similar chasm between the number of women sexually assaulted and the tiny minority who ever see legal justice. The barriers start before women even report such incidents, cultivated by a society that tells us that it's 'just' groping, it was 'just' a joke, it's 'boys being boys', but they persist at every level of the system.

This is frustrating for individual women who are repeatedly barred from the justice they have every right to access, but is even more devastating in the context of a crime we know often escalates from 'low-level' behaviours to more serious forms of abuse. Every woman deterred from reporting represents a miscarriage of justice, not only for herself, but also for an unknown number of other potential future victims. And the unsettling experience of being told you are 'making a fuss', when what has happened to you is actually illegal, can take an enormous mental toll.

Imagine, even if you did reach court, the likelihood (in our society where this crime is so normalised) that you'd be facing a jury on which one or more of the male jurors has quite possibly committed a similar offence themselves and got away with it. If this sounds like an exaggeration, consider a 2021 study examining sexual violence by male UK students. Out of 554 students surveyed, sixty-three of them admitted that they had committed sexual assault, rape or another 'coercive and unwanted incident' in the past two years alone. That is 11 per cent. There are twelve people on a jury, so it's not that far-fetched after all.

Ask yourself how many women you know who have experienced some form of 'unwanted sexual contact'. Groping. Stroking. Touching. Licking. Grabbing. Thrusting. This is absolutely endemic. We just don't call it 'sexual assault'. How likely is it that male jurors, with no legal expertise, will convict someone of sexual assault in a society in which they are reasonably likely to have done the same thing themselves? How likely is it that, at the very least, this will influence their decision-making? And can you think of any other crime in which this would be the case?

So a vanishingly tiny proportion of these cases even reach court in the first place, let alone result in a conviction. And, in turn, the lack of justice helps to reinforce the idea that it isn't really a crime at all.

Injustice at work

Then there are the systemic barriers to justice for those who experience discrimination or harassment in the workplace. Even for those who overcome the pressure to dismiss it as 'banter' or jokes, there is a massive hill to climb to reach any kind of justice. There are the initial, internal mechanisms that can drag on for months and often see victims forced into so-called 'arbitration' with the men who have harassed and assaulted them.

> I raised a sexism and bullying complaint that was 'expertly' drawn out and delayed by the HR department . . . In retrospect, I regret raising the complaints, although they were very justified, because I was treated as 'the enemy' and the complaint process itself was traumatic. I learnt that telling the truth isn't enough and the justice system isn't usually about justice.

Then there is the backlash and retaliation so frequently faced by victims, who find it is their career, not that of the perpetrator, that suffers.

> I was sexually harassed for years and eventually assaulted by a work colleague. When I brought this to the attention of the senior management of a charitable social housing association, nothing was done. When I formalised it in grievances, I was faced with

aggression, antagonism, animosity, bullying, discrimination, victimisation and eventually dismissal from work. Talk about justice and fairness!

Women who are sexually harassed at work are often blamed for not reporting what happens to them. We know that over half of all women and two-thirds of young women are sexually harassed at work, but only around 20 per cent feel able to report the harassment to their employer. Here again we are blaming women when it is the system that is broken. Because, when women *do* report to their employers, guess what? A whopping three-quarters say that nothing changes as a result, while a further 16 per cent say that they are treated worse. In other words, a paltry 9 per cent of women get any positive outcome from reporting their sexual harassment.

Even for the tiny minority of women who make it as far as an employment tribunal, the odds are stacked against them. And I really mean a tiny minority. Consider the fact that over half of all women have experienced sexual harassment, which equates to millions of cases, and then despair at the EHRC's estimate that only fourteen tribunal claims for workplace sexual harassment were made in the year 2018–19.

The structures of tribunals can make it very difficult for victims to access justice. The system allows employees a strict time limit of just a few months from experiencing harassment or discrimination to bring a tribunal case against their employer. For some, the process of steeling themselves and finding the confidence to report may take much longer. For others, particularly in cases of maternity discrimination, the choice of going through an incredibly stressful and expensive tribunal within the first months of their babies' lives is simply no choice at all.

While on maternity leave, I was told in a casual conversation that the man who had been brought in to cover my leave was now going to be promoted above me. I had been in the department for four years and he had been in the company for not even two months . . . I could not afford legal advice and this left me feeling really down and worthless. I did not feel I could go through a tribunal while dealing with two young children and breastfeeding, even if I could afford the legal advice.

In the cases when a firm does admit wrongdoing, there is still a high chance that, if a victim receives any kind of compensation, she will be forced to sign a non-disclosure agreement (NDA), usually forbidding her from ever telling anyone about the discrimination or harassment she experienced and requiring her to pretend she left the company voluntarily. While secrecy surrounding NDAs makes it difficult to gather accurate statistics, we know from charities like Pregnant Then Screwed that their usage is rife – pushing women into an impossible choice between the right to speak out and the money they desperately need, while allowing companies to act as badly as they like and simply pay to keep these incidents quiet.

The most galling thing I have found about losing my career to maternity discrimination is that, as well as losing my job, I've lost a sense of who I am and have been so incapacitated by the stress of the experience that I don't know how to pick myself back up. I have all this anger and hurt that I can't seem to move on from. It's also frustrating that the law makes settlement and NDAs the norm, so I have to carry it alone.

Joeli Brearley, founder of Pregnant Then Screwed, says: 'There are many well-known companies who use [NDAs] regularly to cover up mistreatment of new mothers in the workplace. For obvious reasons, we cannot say the names of these companies, but the public would be very shocked if they knew what was going on behind the closed doors of some of the most well-known and loved brands in the UK.'

The worst part is that NDAs can cover up serial offending if the same company repeatedly discriminates against women but nobody is ever able to reveal that pattern of institutionalised misogyny.

Here, too, are those insidious intersections: when access to justice depends on whether or not you are able to afford it.

A young single mother of two small children describes how, after months of workplace sexual harassment, she was fired by her manager after he attempted to sexually assault her. She wrote, 'I never did anything except look for a new job because I knew, at twenty-two years of age, that I could never afford a lawyer and that he'd just lie if the case ever went to trial.'

Another woman was at an employment tribunal when the male judge and the respondent's barrister started joking about whether 'cunt' and 'tit' were really offensive terms for a woman to be called in the office or just a bit of a joke. She was unrepresented as she could no longer afford to pay for her solicitors. So she had to try, alone, to explain the gendered nature of the slurs. She had been abused and belittled by male colleagues and had learned that men doing the same job were earning five times her salary and took home a bonus 100 times higher. And yet still there she was, desperately trying to point out institutional sexism in a system supposedly designed to give her access to justice.

The systems are not built for us. It is impossible to conclude anything else. And, without bold, root-and-branch reform, they will continue to protect the powerful from redress for discrimination and abuse, instead of enabling the most vulnerable to access justice.

Even when 'justice' is done, the outcome is not always perfect. To argue simply that every man accused of rape or domestic violence should receive much longer and tougher custodial sentences is to ignore the problems with mass incarceration that have been carefully traced in devastating detail by scholars and activists. Studies have suggested that custodial sentences are not necessarily effective in preventing crime or re-offending. They have also been shown to have a higher likelihood of being imposed on vulnerable and minoritised groups. In many countries, notably the US, it is not possible to separate a discussion of a carceral justice system from the institutional racism that this system both demonstrates and exacerbates.

So it is not necessarily about demanding longer prison terms; it is about recognising that our treatment of rape within the justice system is utterly inadequate in comparison to the seriousness and action afforded to other crimes. Realising that the abuse and mistreatment of women at work is so normalised that it occurs with near total impunity.

As we hopefully move towards reform of justice and punishment, we need to ensure that the severity and impact of gendered abuse is fully acknowledged. Whatever form it takes, justice must be made available to victims, instead of remaining frustratingly out of reach.

POLITICS
AND PRIVILEGE

There are further connections here. We cannot look at the criminal justice system in isolation, when it is so heavily influenced by the political sphere. There is no small irony in the fact that the lord chief justice's remarks were made to the House of Lords, an institution of power in which almost three-quarters of peers are men and just 6 per cent come from a minority ethnic background (compared to 13 per cent of the general population). This imbalance persists across political power structures, reflected in the make-up of those who are responsible for voting on or amending new laws, appointing police and crime commissioners, and influencing education policies and priorities.

If the make-up of the House of Commons instead reflected that of the UK population, there would be about ninety-three MPs from ethnic minority backgrounds. There are currently just sixty-five. Women comprise only a third of MPs in the House of

Commons and fewer than a fifth of those who attend cabinet. But, of course, that doesn't necessarily mean that the male members of this overwhelmingly male-dominated sphere aren't alive to the issues and complexities of violence against women and able to put in place effective measures to tackle it.

Except . . .

It is this overwhelmingly white, male-dominated parliament that has left frontline women's services at an absolute crisis point, with hundreds of women and children turned away from lifesaving support because of woeful underfunding. It is this parliament that declined to add any of the provisions for migrant women to the Domestic Abuse Bill that campaigners had begged for, effectively creating a two-tier system in which some survivors are unable to access vital support. It 'consistently failed' to consider gender in its response to COVID-19, according to research from the London School of Economics, which analysed the minutes from seventy-three meetings held in 2020 by the Scientific Advisory Group for Emergencies. This resulted in little government effort to mitigate the enormous gendered impacts of the pandemic, including: working mothers losing their jobs at far higher rates than fathers; new mothers traumatically forced to give birth alone while pubs heaved; massive job losses in the hospitality, retail and service sectors, which hit low-paid women hardest; and pregnant women left unprotected at work, with tragic outcomes such as the death of nurse Mary Agyapong. Even the 'build back better' plan was focused largely on construction projects, despite the fact that research by the Women's Budget Group showed that a similar investment in care could create nearly three times as many jobs, including more roles for women, who are at greater risk of redundancy.

This doesn't mean that women were callously or deliberately

ignored. But it has been revealed again and again that, when a non-diverse group of people are making decisions on behalf of an entire population, the lack of equal representation is likely to result in blind spots. Blind spots like the one that apparently saw the government fail to anticipate the catastrophic upswing in domestic abuse that might occur as a knock-on effect of a national lockdown. After imposing restrictions, it took the Westminster government nineteen days to announce a social media campaign to encourage people to report domestic abuse, as well as an extra £2 million for domestic abuse helplines. In that nearly three-week period, eleven women, two children and one man had already been killed in suspected domestic abuse cases.

Lack of representation also results in the sort of breath-taking political farce that we saw in November 2021 when MPs tried to make it illegal to take non-consensual photos of a woman breast-feeding in public. So far so straightforward, right? Who could possibly object to that? Enter hereditary (unelected) peer Lord Wolfson of Tredegar, who opposed the law in the House of Lords on the basis that it would unfairly criminalise a man, photograph-ing his wife on the beach for his own sexual gratification, if he accidentally caught a breastfeeding woman in the background. No, really.

This is what happens when we have unelected men inheriting the power to influence our laws because of ancient sexist and classist rules: the rights of women to breastfeed without being harassed are sacrificed to the hypothetical sexual gratification of one hypothetical man in a bizarre and extraordinarily unlikely hypothetical situation. As many commentators pointed out, Lord Wolfson's family holiday snaps must be fascinating. But, seriously, if ever there were a more compelling (or ludicrous) example of why it matters that our political system is completely dominated by rich, white men with little knowledge or understanding of the experiences of huge swathes of the population, I'd love to hear it.

Hussein tells me about the surreal and frustrating experience of trying to talk about FGM legislation in a parliamentary evidence session in which the majority of the panel were men. 'We're talking about women's bodies,' she says. 'How do I even talk about FGM when I'm talking to a group of men?'

Nimco Ali has described similarly frustrating experiences, famously relating how the health secretary asked her if she was capable of having an orgasm. 'It depends how good you are, Jeremy,' she quipped.

Defending the new, almost complete ban on abortion in Texas, Governor Greg Abbott said, 'Obviously it provides at least six weeks for a person to be able to get an abortion.' But this revealed total ignorance on his part about the workings of women's bodies and their healthcare, as doctors date pregnancies from the first day of the individual's last menstrual cycle, not from ovulation or conception. This means that many women seeking abortions under the new law would have far less than six weeks to do so – and that's before you even begin to address the fact that, accounting for variations in menstrual cycles, many women simply wouldn't even know they were pregnant by that point.

When asked about the impact of the new law on rape victims, Abbott absurdly responded that 'Texas will work tirelessly to make sure that we eliminate all rapists from the streets of Texas by aggressively going out and arresting them and getting them off the streets'. The suggestion that Texas would prioritise cracking down on rapists because of issues around abortion, rather than because they commit devastating crimes against women (and should have been a priority regardless of the ban), was bad enough. But the statement also demonstrated a complete lack of any awareness or understanding about the nature of rape as a crime. That a rapist is far less likely to be a shadowy stranger on the street than a partner or colleague, a friend or acquaintance. That a woman forced to carry the child of her rapist may also be in a relationship with that man, her potential escape complicated and hampered by an unwanted pregnancy.

Should laws that will devastate women's lives really be enacted by men with no knowledge whatsoever of the consequences of their actions and decisions?

The political climate

Perhaps the greatest irony is that the inability of politicians to recognise the specific experiences of discrimination and abuse faced by women is exacerbated by the fact that women in politics face so much discrimination and abuse that they are underrepresented among decision-makers. Parliament is hostile to MPs who also have caring and family obligations because its practices as a system have barely changed since it was first formed (at a time when women weren't even allowed to vote, let alone become politicians). As an MP, you're expected to split your time between your constituency and Westminster and to be available at all times of day and night for votes, with no working arrangement in place for proxy voting or even proper maternity leave for MPs. This leaves women like Tulip Siddiq and Stella Creasy forced to postpone caesarean sections or gasp their way into parliament battling gestational diabetes while nine months pregnant because it is the only way to ensure they can do their job. And it's almost impossible to get the government to listen or care or do anything about it because – surprise! – they're almost all men and haven't been personally affected by this problem that so many of them don't even seem to realise exists! Vicious circle after vicious circle.

Those women who do battle through the discrimination they face at selection and among voters will then face a barrage of rape and death threats, which have simply become the norm for female politicians. One MP told the BBC: 'I get called a whore, [told] that I'm a slut, that I should put my tits away, that I'm unintelligent, that I'm an idiot, that I should go away and bake a cake instead . . . [They claim] I'm uneducated, I have no place in politics – and you get this daily, it's recurrent.'

The abuse is intersectional. Labour MP Diane Abbott, who receives horrendous misogynistic and racist abuse online, was the target of almost half of all abusive tweets sent to female MPs in the run-up to the 2017 general election. In other words, the MPs from the most underrepresented groups, whose voices we most desperately need in parliament, are also those who are most likely to bear the weight of constant and vitriolic threats.

And yes, you might be shocked to hear that sexual harassment and assault are also reported with troubling regularity by women working in politics. A UK poll found that a fifth of people working in Westminster had faced sexual harassment in the past year alone, with women reporting twice as many incidents as men. But, as in the policing and the legal system, policies and procedures to tackle the problem fall woefully short.

In 2019, after a slew of allegations of rape, sexual harassment and abuse were made against sitting MPs in the wake of the #MeToo movement, politicians promised to fix this broken system that provided few repercussions and very little accountability. An inquiry found that there was institutional impunity in parliament, in which cases had 'long been tolerated and concealed' in a culture of 'deference, subservience, acquiescence and silence'. And, despite some much-trumpeted 'reforms' at the time, those who report sexual harassment are still waiting years for any outcome. It's hard to believe the claims of reform when a Conservative MP, found by an independent panel to have made repeated and unwanted sexual advances towards a member of staff in his office, was recently readmitted to the party. Meanwhile, when both a sitting Conservative MP and a journalist made allegations of inappropriate touching against the prime minister's father (which he denied), the silence from the ruling party was deafening. Nokes, the MP in question, later said that the media had immediately begun to scrutinise her past sex life, trying to find proof that she was 'the sort of woman it's okay to sexually harass', while a fellow MP openly told the press, 'I don't believe it happened.'

It is hard not to conclude that those in positions of power have little grasp of the complexity and breadth of the issue of violence against women and institutionalised misogyny. The UK government's response to the death of Sarah Everard was to propose posting undercover police officers in clubs and increasing the number of CCTV cameras on the streets. These measures will do nothing to tackle the underlying misogynistic attitudes that give rise to abuse in the first place, nor will many women be reassured by the introduction of yet more officers after a police officer himself raped and murdered a young woman against the backdrop of an enormous catalogue of police failings and abuses in the sphere of violence against women. Most significantly of all, these solutions will, once again, focus on so-called isolated incidents. They do nothing to address the systemic elements of the problem.

In 2021, Home Secretary Priti Patel discussed the suggested release of a new app that could log women's movements as they walk home and raise an alarm if they fail to reach their destination. She said, 'This new phone line is exactly the kind of innovative scheme that would be good to get going as soon as we can.' It was a gut punch for the women's organisations that had spent the past year advocating for meaningful, evidence-based solutions, including education, a public-awareness campaign and more focus on perpetrators. There was little to suggest the government were listening. Yet an app from a company with no specialist knowledge of sexual violence, which would once again require self-policing by women while doing nothing to actually prevent assault, immediately caught the ear and the imagination of the home secretary.

Excuse me while I put down the camping-size backpack I've had to bring with me to hold all my 'venturing outside as a woman' gear, which now includes attack alarms, self-defence weapons, drink-testing kits, anti-rape devices, a bus-signalling torch, several pairs of handcuffs, a magnifying glass, and some flat shoes to walk 'safely' home in. I'll just put all that down so I've got my hands free to input my location into the app that will track my movements and alert someone if I don't reach my destination at a specified time. Not that they'll get there in time to stop me from being murdered, mind you. But at least it'll make it nice and easy for the police to find my body. And I'm sure I don't need to worry that this effectively means entering my details into a police-accessible database of women's routes home. Because we can all trust the police never to prey on a lone, vulnerable woman, can't we?

Speaking in the House of Commons in the wake of Sarah Everard's death, Prime Minister Boris Johnson almost seemed to display a grasp of the complex continuum of sexist attitudes and sexual violence when he said, 'We have to address the fundamental issue of the casual everyday sexism and apathy that fails to address the concerns of women – that is the underlying issue.' What he didn't acknowledge, though, was the role he, as a high-profile and influential public figure and former journalist, had played in normalising and encouraging precisely those attitudes in the first place. He who had mocked Muslim women for looking like 'letterboxes' and 'bank robbers'. He who had famously called women 'hot totty', described the children of single mothers as 'ill-raised, ignorant, aggressive and illegitimate', and called for action to 'restore women's desire to be married'. He who suggested that women only go to university to 'find men to marry'. He who criticised 'the modern Briton [for] his reluctance or inability to take control of his woman'. He who wrote that a man faced with his female boss's advice in the workplace should simply 'pat her on the bottom and send her on her way'.

These aren't slips of the tongue or unfortunate turns of phrase. Many of these examples are not off-the-cuff, heat-of-the-moment remarks, but rather carefully considered content Johnson wrote for national newspapers in articles to be read by millions. They reveal a man who knew exactly what he was doing by repeating misogynistic and racist views again and again, often deliberately with the aim of whipping up support from men who share his bigotry – like when he promised that 'voting Tory will cause your wife to have bigger breasts'. Let us not sugar-coat it; this is important. No matter how much Boris's trademark buffoonery might like to undercut its seriousness, this is our prime minister saying things that could absolutely be viewed as an endorsement of coercive control and workplace sexual assault.

It is significant, too, in light of these comments, that Johnson was accused by a journalist of having squeezed her inner thigh under the table at a lunch event. She also said that the woman sitting on Johnson's other side reported exactly the same behaviour. Johnson denied the allegations.

Is this a man who is capable of engaging, in any meaningful sense, with the 'fundamental issue of casual everyday sexism'? Yet it is this man who ultimately gets to determine our national priorities.

This is a system, then, in which women are dramatically underrepresented, in which sexual harassment is common and in which adequate policies to prevent and tackle it are not present. All that remains is to question whether all this impacts the output of our political sphere. Does it have the effect of amplifying inequality externally?

Priorities

In 2021, young women across the UK began to share stories of sexual abuse, rape and severe harassment perpetrated by their school and university peers, often on campus. Their testimonies, collected by Soma Sara, a young woman who started an initiative called Everyone's Invited, soon swelled to 50,000 in number. Their stories, echoing the tens of thousands shared by schoolgirls via the Everyday Sexism Project, made it very clear that sexual violence was a serious threat to the safety, wellbeing and education of girls.

In response, the government professed surprise and consternation. The disclosures were 'shocking and abhorrent', said the then-education secretary, Gavin Williamson. His claims that this was alarming new information were bolstered by the media, which ran salacious front-page stories describing the situation as an 'Elite School Sex Scandal' (rather than a public health crisis of catastrophic gendered abuse, impacting girls across all different types of schools).

Yet the government had known about the epidemic of school sexual violence for years. Its own Women and Equalities Select Committee had published a report on sexual harassment and sexual violence in schools in 2016. The findings laid out clearly and unequivocally that girls were 'consistently reporting high levels of sexual harassment and sexual violence in schools'. The report was packed with both statistics and first-hand accounts illustrating the severity of the problem. It also ended with over thirty recommendations, many of which were not subsequently implemented.

The report urged: 'The government and schools must make tackling sexual harassment and sexual violence an immediate policy priority.' Yet, five years later, the education secretary himself apparently had no idea of the scale of the problem. The truth, of course, was not that the government didn't know. It was that the problem – the sexual assault of one in three teen girls at school and the reporting of an average of one rape per school day from inside schools – was simply not treated as a priority.

> It was in Year 7, that I had my first experience of . . . grossly inappropriate touching and a threat of rape if I told anyone what these two boys in my Year 7 maths class were doing to me, which was horrifying and terrifying.

In the wake of the media attention drawn by Everyone's Invited, Williamson commissioned an Ofsted review and a phone helpline was set up for victims to seek support. Yet relatively few cases were referred to police or even dealt with directly by schools. The vast majority of the girls who had courageously described assaults and abuses saw no justice. The media ran articles lamenting the tarnished futures of promising young men who were falsely accused. 'Is the "name and shame" approach the right one?' asked one such piece. 'And how do schools achieve a balance of letting students make mistakes while keeping all children safe?' Once again, the media machine aligned with other institutions in minimising and belittling sexual violence; in this case, by quietly reducing rape and sexual assault to simple 'mistakes'.

I visited schools where wealthy parents had written urgent and cajoling letters to headteachers, strongly urging them not to 'overreact'. Though they needn't have worried. In practice, despite the exposure of this crisis, very little changed, certainly in the short term.

Also in 2021, news broke that a European Super League in football had been secretly planned as a rival to the UEFA Champions League, bringing together twenty European football clubs. Fans feared that this would harm football, rendering domestic competition irrelevant. The next morning, the 'crisis' in football made almost every single national newspaper front page, with headlines including: 'The Fight for Our Game'; 'Shameful Theft of Our National Sport'; and even 'Now it's War'. It quickly became clear that the super league posed a horrendous and urgent threat. The prime minister immediately began mobilising lawyers and holding meetings with the Football Association, the Premier League and various football fan groups, vowing to do whatever was necessary to stop it. 'No action is off the table and the government is exploring every possibility, including legislative options, to ensure these proposals are stopped.' ITV reported that Johnson had told a round-table meeting that the government should 'drop a legislative bomb' straight away to prevent the league. Whatever else was on his schedule that day must have been pushed aside. Meanwhile, everybody from pundits to royalty leapt to join the condemnation of this atrocity. 'Now more than ever we must protect the entire football community,' tweeted the Duke of Cambridge. Within seventy-two hours of its announcement, the proposed super league had been suspended following the withdrawal of all six Premier League clubs involved. Which really shows what can be achieved when things are considered a 'political priority'.

I make this comparison not to knock football, but because it highlights the level of urgency and importance we as a nation are prepared to designate to two very different topics: the sexual assault and rape of thousands of schoolgirls compared to the act of kicking a ball back and forth across some grass.

MEDIA MISOGYNY

The trends in the portrayal of women in our media both reflect and worsen sexist attitudes. Women are used as window dressing, sexualised and infantilised, from the ongoing mockery of the *Daily Mail*'s endless headlines about women 'flaunting', 'showcasing' and simply owning body parts to the weaponisation of sexism and misogyny against female politicians.

The newspapers we see flapping on an empty seat of the bus, the television murmuring in the background as millions of families have breakfast, the magazines we leaf through at the hairdresser's or in the doctor's waiting room . . .

In all these ways and so many more, the media provides the wallpaper to our daily lives. Its portrayal of women is not just significant, but also formative. When a child sits down to paint on a kitchen table covered in sheets of newspaper and sees men hard at work in suits and women shamelessly used for decoration, they are already learning that men are purposeful and important, while women are ornamental.

But it's more than that. The media doesn't just tell us what to think about women; it also controls how people hear about and perceive our efforts to change things.

When feminist issues make it into the headlines at all, they are often ridiculed and presented as the shrill, unreasonable demands of snobbish, pearl-clutching prudes or lazily entitled, overly 'woke' and ungrateful millennials. This portrayal, which has seen women complaining about workplace sexual harassment labelled 'feminazis' and women who choose to speak out about pressure from the media derided as 'arrogant spoiled brat[s]', feeds into unhelpful stereotypes, reinforcing the already popular idea that gender inequality no longer exists, that feminists are overreacting man-haters, thereby making it much harder to persuade people to participate in positive change.

Women who spoke about their experiences in the wake of the #MeToo campaign, for example, found their stories were often dismissed or disbelieved, with high-profile media outlets questioning whether this was a 'witch hunt' against men and whether 'feminism has gone too far'. In the year following the resurgence of the #MeToo campaign, the percentage of male managers in the US who said they were uncomfortable participating in a common workplace activity with a woman, such as mentoring or working one-on-one, increased by 32 per cent to 60 per cent. This huge shift should not be seen, as many media outlets suggested in their coverage, as a 'backlash' against the women who had shared their stories. That simply doesn't make any sense. For men who have not committed a sexual assault or sexually harassed women at work, women reporting harassment or assault presents no threat. The notion of danger comes instead from media rhetoric that repeatedly implies that all men are at risk from #MeToo and that women are making up lies about men to bring about their downfall. One study found that just 56 per cent of the UK news-paper coverage of #MeToo was positive.

It is also largely the media that has the power to choose whether or not to hold politicians to account and which stories or scandals to cover or ignore. With the power to shape the careers of prime ministers and even swing elections, what newspapers present us goes far beyond just holding up a mirror to society. The media is another powerful system in itself.

All this is closely interconnected. It is difficult to attract more women and girls into politics while female politicians are subjected to weaponised misogyny in the mainstream press. For example, when Scottish First Minister Nicola Sturgeon was portrayed in hyper-sexualised cartoons and variously described as 'Lady Macbeth' in high heels, a baby-killing 'Godzilla' and a 'Little Miss' with 'bigger balls' than her male opponents. Such routine media portrayals open the door to the barrage of online abuse female politicians face on a daily basis. How much easier is it for constituents to click 'send' on a death threat to a female MP when they are fed a regular diet of only marginally more sanitised prejudice and attacks in the mainstream press? Or, indeed, when articles are published ridiculing the very notion that these women might have faced racist and sexist treatment in the first place?

It is almost unbearably frustrating to come up against this complacency, this denial, this blatant, patronising dismissal. I don't know how to describe the sense of jarring dissonance when you step onto yet another daytime TV show to face off against yet another middle-class white man to 'debate' yet again whether feminism has gone too far or whether sexism still exists immediately after having yet another tearful conversation with the make-up artist about a star who used his power and profile to sexually assault her with impunity, or after you were led to the studio by a runner who whispered her story of grinding daily sexism in your ear, or after the wardrobe assistant sat in the green room gripping a mug of tea while telling you her experience, too. I know these women. I have heard their stories. And, moments later, I am put on camera and told I am overreacting by a man who simply can't see what he has never encountered, but none-theless feels confident enough to deny its existence to millions of viewers – many of whom, of course, will have their anti-feminist suspicions and misconceptions comfortably confirmed by his star turn.

In some cases, it is a genuine, if misguided, attempt at jour-nalistic balance. But, too often, the violation of women is simply seen as a game; an opportunity for entertainment. Like when I was kept in a separate dressing room from a Page 3 model before a 'debate' about the printing of photos of topless women in the newspaper so as to 'ramp up the tension', while being egged on by producers who were very clearly hoping for a catfight. Or the time a programme representative raced into the dressing room to offer me a contract to sign just seconds before going on air because the male journalist I was due to 'debate' about whether sexism still exists had discovered at the last moment that he had been offered a fee for his appearance and I had not. How every-body laughed about that. On one daytime television show, I was pitted against a famous radio provocateur who fiercely defended the argument that teenage girls who experience street harassment are 'asking for it' in the way they dress. The moment the cameras stopped rolling, he pumped my hand enthusiastically with a broad grin and patronisingly told me I'd done 'very well' in my attempts to contradict him. To me, having been followed, masturbated at, spat on, grabbed, touched and assaulted in the street from my early teens, it felt like what we were talking about was a matter of physical urgency, in some cases a matter of life and death. For him, I realised in that moment, it was all just a game.

There was a brief period in the autumn of 2021 when it became trendy in the UK media to 'debate' whether violence against women 'should be taken as seriously as terrorism' (or, as the *Daily Mail* subtly put it, 'as seriously as TERRORISM'). Countless headlines mulled the issue and I was asked about it more than once on air. What was staggering was that nobody seemed to recognise how enormously offensive the question was. In the seventeen years from 2003 to 2020, there were ninety-fives deaths in England and Wales due to terrorism (excluding perpetrators). In many other years, the number is zero. Meanwhile, one woman dies every three days at the hands of a man and 1.6 million women experience domestic abuse annually. And here we are, casually debating whether or not we should really take it that seriously.

So, as a campaigner, you are repeatedly faced with a choice that is really no choice at all. Do you accept such invitations and attempt to use the airtime to redirect attention towards the devastating systemic inequality that impacts women's lives every day? Or do you decline, refusing to take part in yet another 'debate' that risks encouraging the audience to think of this as a potentially imaginary issue with two 'equal' viewpoints, thereby missing out on the opportunity to reach that audience altogether? The media has us in a chokehold.

Of course, the media is not a single, homogenous institution. There are some outlets and individuals working hard to expose inequality in the face of a more widely hostile and undermining trend towards reinforcing and even increasing it. But, if we take the sector as a whole, we might still usefully apply the test of whether our media is systemically sexist by looking at its composition, the experiences of the women who work in it, how those experiences are dealt with, and the external impact it has on our society.

We don't have to look far to see the evidence of systemic gender imbalance in the media: at the time of writing, there are just five female editors of national newspapers in the UK, alongside fourteen men. The most recent data, from 2017, found that women write just a quarter of front-page stories, with the study authors noting that progress since their previous audit, five years prior, had been 'slow or non-existent'.

There is ample evidence, too, of women's experiences of sexism and harassment. A UNESCO survey in 2020 found that 73 per cent of women journalists who responded had experienced online violence in the course of their work, with a quarter receiving threats of physical violence and a fifth having been attacked offline in connection with the online violence they had experienced. A UK-specific study of 3,500 respondents working in media and advertising found that a fifth of women aged 18–24 had been sexually harassed within the first few years of working in those industries alone.

The Second Source, an organisation set up by women journalists to tackle harassment in UK media, was inundated with shocking examples from across UK newsrooms, including 'the 22-year-old trainee who was led into a hotel room by a fifty-year-old editor, who said that she needed to strip for a magazine cover on erotic fiction', and 'the manager who sacked a freelancer because he "couldn't deal with his temptation"'.

So does this male-dominated culture in which sexual harassment is common lead to harmful output?

Yes: we can see it in the barrage of sexist media coverage so plentiful that it would be impossible to list it all here. We see it in the selection of stories, views and ideas we are presented with.

A Women in Journalism report found that an overwhelming 84 per cent of front pages featured a male subject or expert. And we see it in wider societal impact, too. A 2018 study revealed that, controlling for other variables, the higher the level of media sexism, the lower the share of women candidates for political office. The study concluded: 'We hypothesise that sexist portrayals of women in the media stifle ambition among women who, in a less sexist media environment, would be willing to stand as political candidates.'

And, at the same time that such treatment is putting women off considering a political career, it is also forcing women out of politics. A significant number of high-profile female MPs who chose to stand down from parliament in 2019 cited sexism and abuse as a factor in their decision. Can all those dudes who tell us women just can't cut it, just aren't as interested in politics, honestly tell us it wouldn't give them pause, when considering a political career, if they knew it might very likely result in national scrutiny of their bodies and cleavage? That they might find themselves on the front page of a newspaper with readers encouraged to compare their legs with those of another woman? Or that they might become the subject of an article simply titled: 'PMQs: whose boobs are these?'?

Misogyny sells

We don't experience these headlines in a vacuum. They jostle for space on the page with glossy adverts that continue to commodify, objectify and hyper-sexualise women, reinforcing the messaging we are absorbing from the text.

You might come across a headline about Johnny Depp's abuse of his ex-wife in the same paper as a massive, brooding photograph of the actor advertising Dior's poorly named 'Sauvage' fragrance. 'I'm being boycotted by Hollywood,' Depp later complained – his claim somewhat undermined by the fact he was lamenting his supposed 'cancellation' from the front page of a major weekend magazine a mere three weeks before he walked the red carpet at another major film festival, promoting his new movie. The newspaper articles read like a parody: 'Johnny Depp has claimed he's become a victim of cancel culture as he prepares to accept the prestigious Donostia Award at the San Sebastian Film Festival.' But remember what we know from the headlines: 'Sexual assault claims destroy the careers of powerful men.'

Then there's the Audi advert that compared women to used cars. Or the chalkboard outside a Belfast pub crowing, 'Ya can beat the wife, but ya can't beat a 5 pound lunch.' As women's careers were decimated by the onslaught of unpaid childcare and domestic labour during the pandemic, you might also have been greeted by an advert from the government subtly reinforcing the idea that such work was indeed 'women's work'. For example, the ad that showed women home-schooling, looking after babies and cleaning the floor, while the only man featured lounged on a sofa.

The problem isn't just the sexist adverts; it is the structural sexism they help to bolster and normalise. The idea of women as sex objects who exist to fulfil men's fantasies. The notion that men are useless in the domestic sphere and simply not suited to childcare or household chores. The harmful belief that changing your body to conform to racist and unrealistic beauty standards is the ultimate achievement for women.

The media is its own sexist ecosystem. But the problem is compounded by the fact that it is also the lens through which every other broken system is presented to us; the lens through which we view education, the police force, the justice system and politics. And, when that lens is not fit for purpose, when it avoids necessary scrutiny, piles objectification on top of underrepresentation and pours petrol on the flames of societal stereotypes, it doesn't just distort the problem; it makes it a hell of a lot worse.

JOINING THE DOTS

If you're not looking for the connections, you might not notice they are there. Once you do start looking, it is impossible to miss them.

In the time it has taken me to write the last section of this book, a family of children jumped out of the window in the middle of the night after a man deliberately rammed an articulated truck into their house in what was described by the press as a 'domestic row'. A man named Jake Davison shot dead five people, including a three-year-old girl, in the worst mass shooting in the UK for more than a decade. Davison was radicalised online, with extensive evidence emerging to show he had been considerably involved with online male-supremacist, woman-hating 'incel' (involuntary celibate) communities. Yet, while the shooting bore all the hallmarks of extremism (an individual radicalised online by a group expressing hatred of a specific demographic group), police immediately declared they weren't even prepared to consider the possibility that the incident could be a form of terrorism.

When violence against women is so normal, how can we see it as extreme?

Labour MP Zarah Sultana has spoken out about a litany of misogynistic, racist and Islamophobic messages, including comments telling her to 'go back to your own country'. 'Muslim women in politics shouldn't have to tolerate this,' she tweeted. When the BBC mistook Labour MP Marsha de Cordova for her colleague, MP Dawn Butler, the *Evening Standard* reported on the story by highlighting the fact that the BBC didn't seem able to tell the difference between two black female politicians. But the *Standard* mistakenly illustrated its own story with a picture of MP Bell Ribeiro-Addy, prompting Ribeiro-Addy to say, 'This ultimately signals that we are not worthy of the same distinction and respect as our white counterparts. I fully understand that mistakes happen, but this is not a unique experience; it has been happening to BAME women MPs for some time.' Meanwhile, Diane Abbott has described in horrifying detail the abuse she experiences, with messages combining racist suggestions about hanging her with the misogynistic caveat of 'if they could find a tree big enough to take the fat bitch's weight'.

The different forms of institutional inequality in our society cannot be neatly separated out under different headings and different 'types' of prejudice, as these experiences show. And, if we try to do so, we not only fail those who live at the intersections of these different forms of inequality, but we also miss vital nuances about the origins of the oppression we are trying to dismantle, which are usually intersectional as well.

It is useless to black women to describe institutionalised misogyny in the police and the justice system without recognising that the same systems are suffused with institutional racism – racism that has been pointed out again and again by campaigners for decades and yet remains denied by the very same political system that continues the cycle of normalising, perpetuating and refuting institutional misogyny.

In 2021, one female police officer told *The Guardian* that there was a culture of 'bravado' and 'toxic masculinity' within policing, which manifested in 'the fetishisation of women, in particular black women'. A report from the Home Affairs Committee the same year found that policing is still heavily unrepresentative: at the current rate of change, the make-up of forces will not match that of the communities they serve for another twenty years (which, as pointed out, would be nearly half a century after the racist murder of Stephen Lawrence). Black people are also 2.4 times more likely than white people to be searched for drug possession, despite being less likely to use drugs. Another 2021 report found that Greater Manchester Police were four times more likely to use force against black people than white people; meanwhile, government figures showed that black people were nine times as likely to be stopped and searched than white people. Prior to this, in 2018, UN human rights experts expressed serious concerns about 'structural racism, over-policing and criminalisation of people of African descent and other minorities in the UK'.

For women who live at the intersection of different forms of prejudice, structural inequalities mesh together in a manner that is cumulative and significantly magnifies impact.

Sandhya Sharma, group coordinator at Safety4Sisters North West, a small frontline feminist black and minority ethnic-led women's charity, gives the example of migrant women, whose abusers 'will always use a woman's immigration status as part of the abuse'. She adds:

Particularly as a migrant woman, [you fear] that you will be removed, that police will lock you up, that you will lose your children and be sent back to your country of origin, so they have an extra and additional horrendous barrier that really prevents them from leaving the relationship and the household. That's key. That's not even looking at interpretation and all the other things that women need, this is just the bare bones. There aren't services available to them – very few refuges will be able to accommodate women with no recourse to public funds: 100 per cent of the women that we saw within the first three months of lockdown were initially refused refuge accommodation when they'd asked for it, so that really shows how stark the situation is.

Elizabeth Jiménez-Yáñez, policy and communications coordinator on violence against women and girls at the Latin American Women's Rights Service, explains how institutional inequality begins to echo and reinforce the violence of abusers themselves:

The perpetrator says, 'Nobody is going to help you,' and then they go to local authorities, they don't help them; they go to social services, they don't get the help; they go to police, they don't get the help. It's a very consistent message that is reinforced in every interaction that these women have with the system.

A young migrant woman who was eligible for a loan during her PhD described how the bank employee in charge of approving her borrowing started 'asking me if I had a boyfriend', talking about his favourite sexual positions and insisting the two of them should 'meet up sometime'. Desperate for the loan, she recalled her 'utter fear' of daring to protest, given the 'different layers of disadvantage he had over me'. He 'played shamelessly', she noted, on the 'twisted power dynamic'.

There is systemic inequality piled on systemic inequality, and the real-life impact is devastating. These systems don't only disadvantage and oppress women and other minoritised groups, but also, in some cases, actively (whether inadvertently or not) help abusers. One woman was beaten bloody by her abuser, leaving her with significant head injuries. But he was so confident in the power and safety that the system gave him to abuse her that he actually drove her to the police station. He taunted her: 'Go on then, choose. Are you reporting or are you staying with me?' She was so terrified to report to the police that she chose to stay with the perpetrator.

At the same time, efforts to tackle only one element of the problem leave many survivors failed and forgotten by the very same systems that amplify such prejudice in the first place. There are the black women who are four times more likely to die in pregnancy or childbirth in the UK, yet who also see themselves least represented in materials for campaigns reaching out to support expectant mothers. There are the disabled women who are twice as likely to experience domestic abuse as non-disabled women, yet also extremely underserved by refuge provision, with just one in ten refuge spaces accessible to those with physical disabilities (23 per cent of women in the UK are disabled). And there are the migrant women whose status often leaves them in a position in which their abuser is in control of their visa or legal processes, yet who face enormous barriers to support from frontline services because they have no recourse to public funds.

Often, too, these intersections result in women being shamefully failed by the very movements supposedly committed to tackling such injustice. The irony is that it is our lists – our interconnected experiences of sexism and abuse, stretching back through our lives – that lead some to argue that trans women should be excluded from the feminist movement. The argument goes that, if they haven't grown up experiencing the bombardment of socialisation, sexualisation, abuse and discrimination that cisgender girls face from birth, they cannot truly understand and have not truly experienced female oppression. But this is ludicrous, partly because no two women's experiences can ever be identical. Many will have been bolstered by forms of protective privilege by nature of their class, race or sheer good fortune, which mean they themselves can never truly understand and have not experienced the same forms of oppression as other women. We do not exclude those women from our movement. We do not demand that everybody prove they have experienced identical histories of oppression in order to be included – except, suddenly, when it comes to trans women. But, perhaps more importantly, it is short-sighted not to recognise that a trans woman has her own list. And, while some of the individual incidents on it may look a bit different (for example: ridicule for transgressively displaying markers of femininity while inhabiting a body designated male at birth; or suffocation in the heavily stereotyped environment of locker-room 'banter' that invalidates and undermines their very existence), it is nonetheless a list of misery and oppression forged by the very same restrictions that affect us all. Yes, it might manifest a little differently, but don't all our histories? To argue that trans youth aren't deeply injured by gender stereotypes, binaries and pressures is surely facetious.

One of the most shocking problems is that we don't really know the scale of abuse faced by those affected by intersecting inequalities – they are often missed out of vital research and their experiences are not captured by official statistics. This makes them even more invisible, pushing lifesaving support still further out of reach. The often-quoted ONS statistics about rape in England and Wales, for example, do not capture abuse experienced by disabled and/or older people in care homes, making their experiences even more likely to be ignored.

Media coverage of the COVID-19 crisis did at least pick up on the disproportionate impact of the pandemic on women's jobs and on the higher rates of death among ethnic minority communities, but rarely did the two themes intersect. Nor was there much attention paid to other overlapping impacts. There was little discussion of the massive impact the pandemic had on disabled women, many of whom endured the double burden of being forced to shield for a longer period of time while coming up against barriers to accessing services, care and essential items – on top of the sudden influx of domestic and childcare responsibilities faced by other women. Nor was much said about the complex issues encountered by mothers of disabled children, for whom the added gendered load was compounded by a massive reduction in the provision of educational and healthcare support.

In a similar way, campaigns surrounding domestic abuse and other gendered issues regularly ignore the experiences and realities of women from the LGBTQ community, and even feminist initiatives, like the highlighting of so-called 'equal pay day' in November (the date when women's wages 'run out' in comparison to men's), fail to capture the reality for women of colour, whose equal pay day, compared to white men, would fall on a much earlier date.

And the intersections are there, too, in the institutional inequality we have been examining.

This might take the form of a police force alleged to have prevented disabled Extinction Rebellion protestors from taking part in further protests by confiscating and impounding aids such as wheelchairs, ramps and accessible toilets. Or a justice system that, instead of taking action against a perpetrator of domestic abuse, investigates the immigration status of the woman reporting him. Or a CPS in which rape victims from an ethnic minority background are significantly less likely to see their case lead to prosecution or conviction.

A society in which black and minoritised women experience higher rates of domestic abuse-related homicide and yet 50 per cent of specialist refuges for black and minoritised women have been forced to close or have been taken over by a larger provider due to lack of funding in the past decade.

A government led by a prime minister who has not only made a string of deeply misogynistic statements, but has also referred to black African people as 'picaninnies' with 'watermelon smiles' and has said of British colonialism in Africa, 'The problem is not that we were once in charge, but that we are not in charge any more.' (All comments he has claimed were satirical or taken out of context.)

But, in the same way that we find it so difficult to recognise the patterns of systemic misogyny, our society also struggles to recognise these connections. We like to think of different problems as neat and compartmentalised, separate and clearly defined. Black History Month here. International Women's Day there. A commission on disability today. An LGBTQ inquiry tomorrow. As though these groups are all mutually exclusive. Which is only a natural assumption if you are taking a straight, white, non-disabled, cisgender, middle-class man as your default 'norm'.

When we begin to recognise these intersections between different systems and between different forms of power and oppression, we can see that, in order to meaningfully tackle oppression in one sphere, awareness of its overlap with others is vital to real progress. That is to say that oppression on the basis of sex cannot be disentangled from colonial oppression or the oppression of indigenous peoples or climate catastrophe or caste systems or harmful religious orthodoxy or poverty or the capitalist commodification that creates grotesque wealth disparity in our world. As Win points out, 'Many of these problems have been worsened by the whole system of capitalism and the global macro-economic system and the militarised world that we live in.'

Indeed, capitalism and patriarchy work together to sexualise and commodify women and then to shame women for that sexualisation, so that they are disempowered, thereby enabling others to capitalise on their sexualisation. Just watch what happens when women have the audacity to take control of their sexuality – the fury and backlash it generates. That's when you can see the connections.

Even when the overlap is horribly apparent – like in Atlanta in 2021 when a young white man massacred eight people, six of whom were women of Asian descent, and told police he was trying to eliminate 'temptation' by launching the attacks at massage parlours as a form of vengeance – even then, we struggle desperately to make the connections. Reporting on the Atlanta incident, one newspaper described 'fears that [the victims] could have been targeted because of their race'. Meanwhile, a police officer told the press that the shooter's actions were 'not racially motivated', but caused by 'sexual addiction'. Yet very few news outlets made the link between the two (with the exception of a handful of opinion writers, most of them Asian American women themselves). Very few of the white, male reporters covering the story drew any link to the fetishisation of Asian women as hyper-submissive sex objects. But, of course, those white, male reporters hadn't lived their lives experiencing this particular intersection of prejudice.

If we can't even see the connections, then the likelihood of tackling them diminishes further still.

FIX THE SYSTEM,
NOT THE WOMEN

Between the second and the third draft of this book, Sabina Nessa died. In the wake of her death, a local council handed out 200 personal safety alarms to women in the area, though they didn't stop men and talk to them about not violently assaulting women. Between the third draft and the copy-edit, we lost Bobbi-Anne McLeod. The male leader of her city's council immediately said, 'Everybody has a responsibility to not put themselves in a compromising position.'

By the time this book is published, it will be another woman's name. Another woman's death. Another man blaming her. We will be saying all the same things again. This is not an isolated incident. It shouldn't be this way.

So how do we fix it? The short answer is that *we* don't.

We have wasted decades telling women and girls how to fix things. How to fix themselves. How to stay safe. It hasn't worked. Because women were never the problem in the first place.

Can you imagine the outrage if we demanded that men take the same precautions we demand of women on a night out? Input your planned route in the tracking app before you set off so that, if you deviate from your route, we can come and check whether you're disposing of a body. Provide a drinks-testing kit because, if you buy a drink for any woman, you're going to be required to prove it isn't spiked. Bring along an alarm to set off if you suspect one of your mates is engaging in inappropriate behaviour. Have your running shoes to hand so that, if you feel an urge to assault someone, you can flag down the nearest bus and swiftly remove yourself from the situation.

When people suggest measures that constrain all women's lives, these are hailed as 'just common sense'. A small price to pay for the luxury of being able to move through the world unassaulted. Women really should travel together after dark. It's just common sense. Just a sensible precaution. We should track them and find out when they are home safe. For their own good, of course.

But when, even in jest, anybody proposes similarly sweeping restrictions to men's freedoms, the #NotAllMen crowd go absolutely berserk. All hell breaks loose. A curfew for men? You must be joking! An outrageous assault on our civil liberties! And, naturally, the manosphere will spin even the most satirical suggestions straight into anti-feminist gold. See how they're trying to muzzle and castrate us? They won't rest until men's rights have all been stripped away! Join the fight against feminism now, before it's too late!

But what about women's liberty, effectively curtailed by an unofficial curfew that means we cannot go out after dark without taking precautions, without feeling scared, without running the risk that we might be the next Sarah or Sabina? What about our lives shrinking smaller and smaller and smaller while 99 per cent of the men who rape us walk free?

And what about the fact that some versions of these measures, if anyone ever dreamed of applying them to perpetrators, might actually work? Unlike the tracking app that would do nothing to protect victims in the moment they were attacked, a similar scheme that tracked the movements of men previously convicted of, say, stalking or serial domestic abuse might actually prevent women's deaths in future. Instead of demanding an invasive and irrelevant search and confiscation of the phones of rape victims, what about spot checks of the WhatsApp messages on police officers' phones to detect the kind of groups dedicated to misogynistic, racist banter that Couzens and his colleagues were allegedly members of?

When girls are denied their right to education because they're told that their skirts might distract male classmates or make male teachers uncomfortable, the girls' adolescent knees are not the problem.

When it is implied that a woman lost out on a promotion because her skirt is deemed unprofessional or unworthy of respect from her colleagues, it isn't her clothes that we need to worry about.

When a woman is raped and we blame the length of her skirt instead of the actions of the man who assaulted her, justice is broken.

When a media mob hounds a young woman in pursuit of up-skirt photographs on her eighteenth birthday, it isn't her choices that need re-examination.

It's not the skirt. It's the system.

The single most important thing to recognise is this: if the problem is systemic, the solution must be systemic. We need structural change. We need to tackle patriarchal structures and deeply ingrained inequality. We need to root out institutionalised misogyny, racism, ableism, ageism, homophobia, classism and other forms of oppression that are built into the very foundations of our society. We have spent hundreds of years telling individual women to change, to be better, more demure, more careful, more intelligent, more courageous, but none of these individualised solutions have worked. Because women aren't the problem.

Six years of rape, sexual assault, physical and emotional abuse because, 'I can do what I want to you – you are my wife.'

No support from police because, 'It's not our problem.' 'It's your word against his – and who would believe a hysterical woman?'

No support from the law because, 'You can't afford us.' 'He has a good lawyer.' 'You would not survive court – they would tear you to shreds.'

No support from family because, 'You must be exaggerating – where are the bruises?' 'You are selfish for leaving and taking your child away from a comfortable home and good father.'

No support from (ex-)'friends' because, 'You probably deserved it – you must have provoked him.'

No support from society because, 'All single mothers are sluts who get pregnant to get benefits and housing.'

No support from the hospital because, 'You are making a fuss about nothing.'

No help from GPs because, 'What have you got to be depressed about, you silly girl?' 'Stop crying and pull yourself together.'

No more support from the fabulous Rape Crisis because, 'We're so sorry – our funding's been cut.'

Global misogyny

This structural discrimination is not confined to any one country. It extends from senior Australian firefighters (speaking out about the systemic misogyny, sexual assault and harassment they have endured throughout their careers) to a Royal Canadian Mounted Police officer (whose Everyday Sexism Project entry described her being raped by a male colleague after he drove her home from a social event). It shows up in Ecuador, where a police officer faces abuse from superiors and co-workers alike, and in Germany, where a model in a cycle helmet and underwear is used by the transport ministry to promote bike safety. Or, indeed, in China, where, at the time of writing, professional tennis player Peng Shuai seems to have disappeared without trace after making sexual assault allegations against a top government official.

A survey of women journalists at African news organisations reveals that half have been sexually harassed at work, presenting 'a significant impediment to a healthy media industry'. In 2021, a judge in Switzerland reduced a convicted rapist's prison sentence on the basis that the rape only lasted eleven minutes and that the victim had not been severely injured. A judge in India in the same year asked a man who had raped a schoolgirl if he would like to avoid jail by marrying her. A judge in Peru acquitted an accused rapist in 2020 because the complainant was wearing red underwear, which he said suggested she was willing to have sex. In Afghanistan, female judges have been hunted by the murderers they convicted after the Taliban took control and released thousands from prison.

Worldwide, laws still criminalise women for extramarital affairs, require male witnesses to testify to rape, condone spousal sexual violence, prevent women from driving or from travelling without a male chaperone and impose countless more restrictions on female freedom and equality. Millions of baby girls are missing because of femicide. Rape is used as a weapon of war.

The systemic connections are always there, if we are not too distracted by blaming individual women to look for them.

In the US, for example: there are estimated to be hundreds of thousands of untested rape kits currently sitting in police storage across the country; research suggests that up to 40 per cent of police officer families experience domestic violence, as opposed to 10 per cent of the general population; and fewer than 1 per cent of rapes lead to felony convictions.

In Australia, a recent flood of allegations of sexual harassment, assault and rape within politics have exposed a system in which powerful men protect their own. From rape accusations against a cabinet minister to a woman's account of rape within Parliament House, as well as an MP's description of a sexist culture that supposedly included being inappropriately touched by a male MP, a powerful picture has been painted of victims ignored, dismissed and disbelieved. Survivors have talked about 'cover-up culture and abuse of power', referencing a system that has failed and silenced them. But it is difficult to challenge this system when you have people as powerful as a defence minister describing one of the alleged rape survivors as a 'lying cow'. And, of course, this doesn't happen in isolation: it's part of a much wider picture. In Australia, 60 per cent of young women say that they have faced gender inequality of some kind. This is also a country in which Indigenous women and girls are thirty-five times more likely to be hospitalised due to family violence-related assaults than other women and girls, but the intersections, as ever, are often missed. Indeed, it has been pointed out that gendered violence is ingrained in colonial history – the same history that condoned the murder, rape and sexual abuse of Indigenous women – yet the summits and initiatives supposedly aimed at improving women's safety fail to address the specific needs of First Nations people.

The picture in other countries is different, but there is no single country that has successfully prevented the most serious forms of violence and abuse against women. There is no country on earth in which systemic gender inequality has been left in the past. And what underpins this inequality is the same in the UK as it is in South Africa, India, Canada or Russia. It is about the fundamental value we place on women. When we value women less, everything else follows.

I am nineteen years old from Benghazi, Libya. I have been reading and learning more and more about feminism and sexism and, the more I do, the clearer it is to me how unfair I have been treated in the past because it was just what everyone thought was normal and okay. When I first started experiencing men catcalling me in the streets (I was probably thirteen), my mother told me I should never look at the man or respond or even defend myself if he tried to touch me because he might get angry and hurt me . . . Early on, I was taught to always cover up; my dad would send me back to my room to change because my pants were 'too tight' and I hated my body because I didn't want to be a sex object . . . My uncle told me it was my job to sacrifice and compromise because that's what a good mother does for her family. I saw my aunt thanking her husband for holding the baby like he was doing her a favour by taking care of his own child. In Libya, we have tribes and these 'important' tribe meetings that women are obviously not invited to because, well, because they're women. I have a cousin who would ignore me every time we met; he would shake hands with everyone in the room but me. I never knew why, but I figured that, if I was a man, it surely wouldn't have happened. When you're a girl, you're automatically less important – easy to ignore.

In the UK in 2019, a businessman subjected his ex-wife to an extended violent assault after discovering she was dating a new man. He attacked her in the car park outside a gym, smashing her head against a BMW so hard that it dented the bodywork, and left her needing hospital treatment. At Stockport Magistrates Court, he was convicted of both assault by beating and criminal damage. He was ordered to pay his ex-wife £150 compensation; he was ordered to pay the owner of the BMW £818.

In Texas, the new abortion law that came into force in 2021 gives women fewer rights than a corpse. The state dictates that a dead person who, while alive, did not consent to the donation of their organs will see their wishes respected, even if a child were dying for need of an immediate transplant. The same bodily autonomy is no longer granted to women in the same state who wish to make their own decisions about their reproductive organs. The debate around abortion is not focused on whether or not a foetus is considered fully human; it is really about whether or not women are.

As Win tells me: 'Women are seen as dispensable. We may not want to accept it, but there you have it. Femaleness is an obstacle course we navigate daily. The enemy is patriarchy and the attendant systems within the state and religious institutions and wider society, which do not see us as humans.'

Win powerfully describes the impact this has on our whole lives. She talks about a tradition in certain African communities she has worked with in which the birth of a baby boy is celebrated with a gun salute 'to announce that an heir has arrived', but the birth of a girl is greeted with silence. (I think back to the ugly gold heirloom.) 'These things stay with you throughout your life,' she says.

> So, by the time you get to femicide, by the time you get to being denied a passport and the chance to travel without a male escort, by the time you get to, as a widow, your property being taken away from you because you are female, etc., etc. . . . It just didn't start on that Monday morning at the University of Zimbabwe when they are denying you registration in the Faculty of Medicine, right? It started with the three-gun salute. And, throughout that journey, there are steps along the way and there are rituals and ceremonies and messages – in the home, in the church, in the mosque, under the tree, in the community – that keep reinforcing this message that you are less important than males, that you exist for the pleasure of the males sexually, that you are here to reproduce.

Hussein echoes her words: 'The moment you're born as a girl, you're at risk of being violated, raped, discriminated against, not getting the right jobs, not getting paid the same as men . . . being told your body is never perfect.'

This is not normal, you know. We need to say this to each other over and over again. We need to tell each other our stories, we need to mourn and grieve and be furious and we need to remind ourselves that this is not the way things should be. Because the greatest threat to our future isn't the abuse and oppression we have suffered; it is the insistence that it never really happened at all.

This does not mean that all women are helpless, cowering, damaged victims. It means that many of us – a majority of us – are survivors. And to claim that is not to enter a state of perpetual victimhood or to give up. It is quite the opposite. It means acknowledging and celebrating the strength, courage and resilience that have brought us this far, releasing ourselves from the internalised blame and shame that we have been forced to carry, and allowing ourselves to see that it really isn't *us*.

> I wanted to finally say all this out loud and to recognise that the endless sexism that I've grown up with shapes lives. I never felt any of it was bad enough to report and was just 'men being men'. I've never connected all these incidences together before and only recently realised that the impact they had upon me has shaped my entire life.

There is massive, world-shaking power in the sharing of our stories. Since I started the Everyday Sexism Project ten years ago, the impact it has had is testament to the power of storytelling. It has contributed to adding consent to the school curriculum, transforming the British Transport Police's approach to sexual violence and changing Facebook's global policies on sexually violent content. It is proof that raising our voices collectively really can bring about concrete progress. It is encouragement to keep going.

Solutions

It is not enough, of course, for women to name and render visible our oppression. 'What's the solution?' people ask. Those who experience systemic oppression are frequently the ones of whom answers are demanded. I cannot count the number of reviews I have read that deride feminist books for failing to offer a magical answer. The articles sneering, 'Did #MeToo really change anything?' – as though the women who courageously spoke out about their own abuse after years of silencing and shame, at enormous personal cost, are somehow failures and their movement useless if the problem cannot be miraculously fixed by them testifying to it. Indeed, the act of forcing people to acknowledge the problem is actually a huge, foundational part of the journey to fixing it.

It is too much to demand that those bearing witness to their own trauma and abuse also present trite, simplistic fixes on a gold platter. The whole point of all this is that the power and the problem lie in institutions, in vast societal structures and political systems. There is no simple answer to how these systems should be dismantled or rebuilt. If there were, if it weren't messy and complicated and frustrating, it would already have been fixed by now.

But, as it happens, women and oppressed people have been suggesting solutions for decades. They just aren't often listened to.

There are the obvious things – the solutions so clear and evidence-based that the fact they have not already been implemented can only be evidence of a lack of will: ring-fenced, sustainable funding for frontline sexual and domestic violence services; an end to the postcode lottery for support; backing for specialist services provided by and for black and minoritised women . . .

Training for teachers to better tackle sexual harassment and misogyny in classroom settings; well-funded education programmes to confront messages from pornography and harmful rape myths in schools; an absolute focus on teaching all children about sexual consent and healthy relationships; a mandatory reporting system for schools and universities to keep track of sexual violence in education . . .

An investigation into institutionalised misogyny and racism across the police and criminal justice system; legal support and advocacy for survivors of rape and domestic violence; mandatory training for police officers to tackle victim-blaming; an end to the invasive and traumatic process of confiscating rape victims' phones or using their sexual history against them in court . . .

A legal requirement for every business, organisation, university and school to have clear, victim-centred policies on sexual harassment and assault; an independent body tasked with overseeing their implementation; media guidelines covering the reporting of sexual offences and domestic abuse; a watchdog with the teeth to take meaningful action when the rules are broken . . .

Complete reform of the House of Lords; implementation of programmes and policies to increase diversity among our political representatives; significant change to the antiquated systems that make parliament a hostile environment for parents and for women . . .

Recording misogyny as a hate crime; a childcare system that is affordable and actually works for working parents; mandatory labelling of airbrushed imagery . . .

But that is just scratching the surface.

When the fickle spotlight of public attention swings briefly towards misogyny and violence against women, as it did in the wake of Sarah Everard's death, there is a tendency for people to respond as though this is the first time anyone has ever considered possible solutions. 'We'll come up with something!' the government cries, shortly emerging with the brilliant plan of placing extra undercover cops in nightclubs. 'We'll treat this as an absolute priority!' the police force promises, before proudly presenting its ideas about how women could flag down a bus.

What all this misses is that the solutions – real, ambitious, systemic solutions that actually match the complex and intersectional nature of the problem – already exist.

They are sitting there, ignored and unused, in the reports and campaign materials of feminist and civil rights organisations, forged through decades of hard work and expertise, created on a shoestring budget and in the face of enormous political and societal opposition. There are already brilliant, clear solutions on offer for each individual link in the chain. Simply acting on some of those would be a start.

There is the forensic, meticulous report into the effective decriminalisation of rape by a group of feminist organisations including Rape Crisis and the Centre for Women's Justice. Its suggestions are balanced, detailed and based on decades of evidence and real women's experiences: review the way the CPS makes decisions in rape cases; give survivors who report to the police the choice of a specialist trained officer; review cross-examination rules; launch a special commission to investigate the use of juries in rape trials and look at whether a different approach might be fairer.

There are the solutions to interlinked racism and misogyny suggested by UK-based black feminist organisation Imkaan: a new law to criminalise sexual harassment, with clear guidance to ensure it isn't implemented in a way that targets particular minoritised communities; specific legislative measures to address racialised experiences of sexual harassment and other forms of violence against women and girls; an end to data-sharing policies when migrant victims approach the police.

Then there is the support for migrant women outlined by the StepUp Migrant Women coalition. And the Women in Prison campaign, fighting to end the incarceration of pregnant women, as well as the Women for Refugee Women campaign, working to end the detention of women who are often survivors of sexual violence and find themselves locked up for months, despite having committed no crime. There are also the solutions to online abuse suggested by feminist charity Glitch, like ring-fencing part of the 'tech tax' on big social media companies to use for funding anti-abuse initiatives.

We also have the Women's Budget Group's alternative economic policies, designed to promote gender equality and tackle the problem of invisible, unpaid women's labour by investing in social care, childcare, healthcare and housing, and refocusing fiscal and monetary policy on building a caring economy.

We can look, too, at the campaigning organisation Pregnant Then Screwed and its recommendations to fix the childcare crisis: expanding flexible working; stopping the use of NDAs as a way of gagging staff who have experienced maternity discrimination; increasing the timeframe within which to raise a tribunal claim from three months to six; offering three months' protected parental leave for both parents; creating properly subsidised childcare from when a child is six months old; making childcare work for those on Universal Credit.

The list goes on and on . . .

All resources the government could draw on in an instant if those with the power to do so chose to pick up and read any one of these reports instead of throwing out ill-conceived, ignorant or apparently spur-of-the-moment suggestions.

But the decisions about how to tackle these challenging, systemic problems are in the hands of men like the MP who told the *Financial Times* there was no way he could be a politician without 'outside interests' (aka lucrative second jobs) because, 'My wife works full time, I've got kids and need the money for childcare.' Yes, there are men who honestly think that, if they can't afford childcare on a salary of £82,000, the solution is to neglect their constituents by taking a cushy role at a firm probably looking for influence in parliament, rather than recognising the systemic crisis that will be impacting poorer families in much more devastating ways than theirs and maybe – just maybe – using their power to do something about it.

These reports and recommendations are not sexy and attention-grabbing. They are complicated and sometimes dull. But that's the point. It's not going to be 200 attack alarms or a handful of new CCTV cameras that will fix this.

And yes, these systemic shifts will require investment, but it is an investment that will bring massive returns. The annual social and economic cost of domestic abuse is estimated at approximately £66 billion in the UK alone. Investment in early childhood education and care brings double the returns. Companies with a more diverse workforce are repeatedly shown to perform dramatically better financially. Empowering women and offering them economic independence dramatically grows economies and leads to other positive development outcomes.

And, even if it didn't, can we perhaps be bold enough for a moment to imagine a world in which we don't need a clear financial incentive to treat women and girls as human beings? To see the global pandemic of violence against women as deserving enough of our money, whether solving the problem brings financial returns or not?

The framework, scope and ambition of this solution would have to be so vast, so interconnected, that one feels daunted just imagining it. Except that you don't have to imagine it. It already exists. You just have to ratify it. The Istanbul Convention – one of the most comprehensive and progressive pieces of legislation ever to address violence against women and girls – recognises the connections between domestic violence, rape, sexual assault, FGM, so-called honour-based violence and forced marriage. It mandates a joined-up approach, including prevention, provision of frontline services, effective prosecution of offenders and independent monitoring of states' obligations. The UK government signed the convention in 2012. A decade later, it is still dragging its feet over ratification, perhaps because it would like to avoid the increased accountability the convention would bring. Yet again, the tools are there, but there is a lack of political will to use them.

And, even when there is political will, even when there is talk about fixing the problem, our targets are pitiful. In a rare moment of acknowledgement, the government's recent rape review saw ministers apologise unreservedly to victims, saying they are 'deeply ashamed' that so many thousands of survivors have been let down by systemic failings. But the so-called 'sweeping reforms' the government has promised to introduce to tackle the problem only aim to restore rates of charging and summons to '2016 levels'. In other words, even in the best-case scenario, we are still looking at significantly fewer than one in ten women who report a rape to police ever seeing justice. That doesn't sound like the system we should be aiming for to me. And even that unambitious target won't be achieved for almost two decades, analysis of the subsequent progress has suggested. There is so little appetite for change. And, if it comes at all, it is glacial, leaving millions of women to suffer while we wait.

Barriers

Then there are social attitudes and cultural norms. There is no legal or policing fix that can work without a shift in the ingrained, normalised misogyny that runs deep in our public consciousness. Sure, we can make it illegal to sack a pregnant woman, but – as long as only 32 per cent of employers believe that statutory maternity rights are reasonable and over a quarter believe that pregnancy puts an unreasonable cost burden on the workplace – we're never going to see those laws cut through in practice. One in nine women will continue to lose their jobs just because they get pregnant.

A 2018 YouGov poll showed that a third of people in Britain think it isn't usually rape if a woman is pressured into having sex but there is no physical violence. A third of men think that, if a woman has flirted on a date, it generally wouldn't count as rape, even if she hasn't explicitly consented to sex. A third of men also believe that a woman can't change her mind after sex has started. Almost a quarter think that sex without consent in long-term relationships is usually not rape. And 40 per cent think it is never or usually not rape to remove a condom without a partner's consent.

As Simon says: 'We will never police our way out of violence against women, so the need to educate younger people and address the underlying issues of harmful gender norms, sexism and misogyny remain some of the most important things we can do now.'

Even this task, daunting as it seems, is not insurmountable. Changing people's minds is difficult, but it has been done before. The government's 'THINK!' road safety campaign correlated with a 46 per cent drop in UK road deaths between 2000 and 2010. A government campaign about sensible drinking between 1989 and 1994 saw a 300 per cent rise in the public's understanding of alcohol units. And research has attributed 13.5 per cent of the decline in smoking prevalence between 2002 and 2009 to tobacco-control mass-media campaigns. When there is willingness to invest both government finance and focus, dramatic results can be achieved. And this is without even factoring in the potential impact of a government-mandated, whole-school educational approach that could transform young people's ideas and misconceptions about relationships and sexual violence.

But, when powerful people and institutions want to avoid being held accountable for a problem that will be costly and difficult to fix, they try to blame it on the choices of individuals. This isn't only something that has happened to women: think of poverty or climate change, for example.

And, when people talk about 'individual choice', I think of Lisa Squire, the mother of Libby Squire. I think about how she might feel when people say that there's no such thing as systemic sexism and that women should just look after themselves better. Two years after Libby was raped and murdered, Lisa's younger daughter, Beth, was 'spiked' by a needle on a night out. Imagine telling Lisa Squire that there's no systemic issue, that this was just a random coincidence. Isolated incidents.

'Keep your eye on where the power is,' Gloria Steinem once told me. It was the best piece of feminist advice I've ever been given.

What can I do?

The chances are, if you are a woman reading this book, you will still be asking, 'But what can I do?' Because, in spite of the overwhelming evidence that this is not our mess to clean up, society has entrenched in us the urge to clean up other people's messes. And there is power in taking action. In not feeling helpless in the face of our own oppression. So yes, while we campaign for the institutional shift we need to see, while we hold power accountable, there are still things we as individuals, of all genders, can do.

First, let yourself make your list. Acknowledge your experiences. Allowing ourselves this acknowledgement, says Mort, may be very painful. It is not a simple or an easy thing to recognise the extent of your own oppression. It will be hard. It might make you feel sad, shocked, furious or hurt. But it is important. It will restore ownership of your own experiences, including the ones that have been taken away from you through shame or disbelief or violence. It will let you recognise that these things have not been your fault. It might let you begin to feel the ways in which their legacy has shaped your life.

It might mean unpicking the layers of denial we have wrapped ourselves in over the years, as a survival mechanism. The patterns we've covered up for so long can be difficult to see.

Mort urges self-care. 'Make the list at your own pace. Do not rush. Take breaks whenever you feel overwhelmed . . . If you find that taking breaks, using coping strategies and sharing with supportive friends is not enough to help soothe you and your distress is ongoing, please seek professional help.' She adds:

> When we start to see the world more clearly, it can be overwhelming. When we allow emotions previously denied to rise to the surface, it can be the same. However, with the right support to feel safe again . . . being fully aware of our lives and the world can be a positive. It can stop us from living on autopilot, from shaming ourselves for what happens to us. It can stop us from numbing out or playing small. And, importantly, this kind of awakening can mean that more and more of us will be inspired

to join our voices and collective resources in order to fight to stop misogyny and other forms of oppression in the future.

This collective action is powerful and vital. When I ask Win what has 'worked' in the course of her long and incredibly effective career as a feminist campaigner, she highlights the importance of 'movements, collectives of women, of social justice activists, working together to make change happen'. Policy shift and global development goals, she says, while useful, only represent a minority of the leverage we need to create real change. 'Nothing takes the place of door-to-door, person-to-person [communication].'

She emphasises the importance of organising across different sectors and bringing together campaigners with different skills and areas of focus. 'We're talking about patriarchy, but we're also talking about white supremacy and capitalism and other forms of oppression and exploitation . . . How do we take on these different things that are so connected?' Even in progressive movements, she warns, there are risks of applying a single-issue lens. It is difficult, she says, to get people, particularly white people working in international development, to recognise the overlap between colonial violence and women's oppression and to join the dots between global manifestations of oppression.

'Historically, development has always been conceptualised as the "civilising mission", from north to south. It was one-way. And the people with the problems and the people with the things that we need to change are "over here". Which is why a lot of NGOs in particular struggle. When you say to them, "You need to talk about what's happening in Europe," they're like, "Oh no, we're going to lose all our supporters . . . [they] don't give us money to talk about what's happening in the UK, we're not domestic players, we are international." We need to acknowledge what is happening in our own backyard.'

Quilliam urges us to recognise the huge progress we are making simply by having these conversations. 'In terms of having it out in the open . . . we are lightyears ahead. And there are lightyears to go. There's a long way to go, but we have come a long way and I can see hope that we can go a long way in the future,' she tells me.

'We need to be prepared for conversations that may not be comfortable. The conversation the Everyday Sexism Project started ten years ago has not been a comfortable one for many people. For those who have revealed what they've suffered, for those who have been called to account for what they've suffered – it's never been comfortable, but we need to be prepared to have difficult conversations. The most important thing is to have the courage to have the conversations.'

And, Win says, don't be scared of backlash: 'If you're doing any work that challenges power and you don't get resistance, then you must ask yourself whether you're actually being effective. If you don't get any pushback, you should know that you are not. You are not really challenging, in my opinion.' She gives a wicked grin: 'You are just singing Kumbaya.'

There is work here, too, specifically for men. The patriarchy puts men in a uniquely powerful position to be the ones to fix the problem. They are granted authority and power that is not accorded to women. And, to state the obvious, they are the ones doing almost all of the attacking and raping and murdering. So it is extraordinary that our society has, for so long, made us believe it is the women's problem to fix.

An attitude shift won't come from awareness campaigns alone and it won't come from women either – not while an entire generation of young men is being conditioned online to see us as whining, man-hating harpies and brainwashed to think of feminism as a conspiracy theory designed to ruin their lives.

This is where men need to step up. With their friends. With their sons. At work. In the locker room. Down the pub. On the pitch. In the streets. When they see it. When someone says it. When they hear about it. When nobody has said anything at all and it's difficult and awkward and uncomfortable.

And, if it's hard to talk about it, imagine what it's like to live it. How we raise our kids matters.

For centuries, we have raised our girls to believe they must keep quiet, behave, not make a fuss. Just look at how this thirteen-year-old has learned to apologise, to blame herself, even in the face of extreme abuse.

> Okay, I hope I don't upset anyone, but [I'm] really self-conscious. We were in drama and a bunch of boys said that they want me to suck their cock and then they followed me home after the lesson, each touching my breasts and my thighs. I told them to stop, but then they said that no one would believe me if I told them because I'm too ugly to be raped. I have tried extremely hard to lose weight as I am the fattest and ugliest out of all my friends. I am sorry if I offend anyone; I'm thirteen, by the way.

We have taught our boys the opposite. Trained them to be powerful, to subjugate, to prove their masculinity by controlling and dominating women.

I am a 28-year-old man. I am just starting to realise how sexist I have been. I have sexually harassed, pressured and even assaulted women throughout my lifetime. I would have never defined the things I have done as this before. I am learning that, in none of my relationships, I have treated women as equal. I have viewed them as my property . . . I honestly believed that this was normal. I remember hearing growing up constantly that being a man was superior in many different ways and that a woman's role was only to bear children and to take care of the household. I spent most of my life up to this point subconsciously trying to impress my father and live up to the values that were passed down to me – to treat women poorly and use them.

It is time to stop. Time to let our girls learn they have nobody to apologise to and nothing to be ashamed of. Time to raise our boys to disrupt the system.

It can be so powerful to allow ourselves to realise, perhaps for the first time, that these things are real, they are unacceptable and, in many cases, they are illegal – and we don't have to put up and shut up any more. It isn't our responsibility to stop this. Society and its institutions and structures have to change. But sometimes this realisation can lead to a huge shift in how we feel – to being empowered, for the first time, to speak up or shout back. And that can be really cathartic, too.

After I was raped during my senior year of high school, I was too terrified and ashamed to speak about it. I developed a drug dependency and, much later, was diagnosed with PTSD. I kept my experience bottled up for nearly two years until, during recovery from my addiction, I reached out to my mom and told her about my experience. She confessed to me that she, too, had been raped in her early twenties and that my grandmother had been the victim of sexual assault and had never spoken about it until my mom reached out to her for support years after her own assault . . . Three generations of women in my family are rape survivors and none of us felt as though we could come forward for the same reasons. I am of the mind that all women have experienced sexism in one way or another, and the idea that women should keep their complaints about everyday sexism to themselves merely perpetuates a culture that places shame and guilt on survivors of sexualised violence and further enables the male social privilege that allows men to get away with acts of sexualised violence. The most important weapon we have as women is our voices, and the communities we create by using them to share our experiences are stronger than we can imagine.

Another example is a sixty-year-old woman who described a lifetime of indecent exposure, using her old diaries to find the details. She listed ten separate offences in all. The first time it happened, she was a schoolgirl on a trip to the seaside, frozen in terror. The last time, some forty years later, 'I told him loudly, clearly, that nobody wanted to see his tiny dick. I finally managed to say it. It felt fantastic.'

Perhaps the most heart-breaking statistics I have come across while researching this book are these two: the majority of women only stand for political office because somebody else asks them to (75 per cent, compared to 54 per cent of men); and the number-one reason women report sexual violence to the police is to stop it happening to someone else.

For years, I thought it was my fault. That day caused me trauma
I didn't know I had; I matured at a rate that no child should.

Afraid of relationships, scared of seeing that boy again. And, if I have any wish, it would be for nobody ever to experience what I experienced that day. It pains me to think that this is normal behaviour and similar and worse instances happen to girls and women daily.

In other words, we only take action to protect other women. What better example is there of our collective internalisation of the messages we are bombarded with? Don't make a fuss. It's not about you. Don't be bossy. Don't be a drama queen. Looking after others is your role. Do what you're told. Be a good girl. Smile, darling.

Of course, there are very good reasons for us to want to prevent another generation from going through this oppression, trauma and abuse.

When I was thirty-seven, I was on the bus with my young daughter and an older, drunk man started to masturbate while looking at us – I cannot bring myself to think about which of us he found so inviting. It made me realise that my daughter's life of sexual-based violence has already started.

It is noble and natural for us to fight because we want to protect our daughters. But let's also fight for ourselves. Let us demand systemic change and reject individual blame for our own sake. For our own futures. For the peace we deserve. For the right to be free.

ACKNOWLEDGEMENTS

This book would not exist without the insight, kindness and support of my brilliant agent, Abigail Bergstrom.

I'm very grateful to my fantastic editors, Fritha Saunders and Assallah Tahir, and all the wonderful team at Simon & Schuster, especially Polly Osborn, publicist extraordinaire, and the brilliant marketing and design teams. Thank you to my eagle-eyed copy-editor, Melissa Bond, whose thoroughness and precision are unrivalled, and to my excellent proofreader Victoria Denne – any remaining mistakes are all mine!

I am indebted to the work of Karen Ingala Smith and the Femicide Census, without which we would not know many of the names listed in this book.

Thank you, Lucy, for being that first small, steady voice of rebellion, and for all that you helped to spark.

A huge thank you to all the interviewees who shared their time and expertise so generously with me.

Thank you to my endlessly supportive mum, my lifeline every

day. Without her encouragement I never would have started and without her guidance and her love I never would have finished.

I am thankful for the work of the warrior women who have been questioning systemic failings, working at the coalface and battling sexual violence for decades, and inspired by the young activists who are springing up with courage and curiosity to follow in their footsteps.

Finally, I am enormously grateful to every one of the 200,000 people who have so courageously shared their stories with the Everyday Sexism Project over the past decade. Our voices are loudest when we raise them together.

HELP AND SUPPORT

Rape Crisis England and Wales
rapecrisis.org.uk Helpline: 0808 802 9999
Frontline-specialised, independent and confidential support
services for women and girls of all ages who have experienced
any form of sexual violence at any time in their lives.

Survivors UK
survivorsuk.org Text helpline: 020 3322 1860
Information, support and counselling for men and boys who
have been raped or sexually abused.

Refuge
refuge.org.uk Helpline: 0808 2000 247
Help for women and children facing domestic violence.

Men's Advice Line
mensadviceline.org.uk Helpline: 0808 801 0327
Advice and support for men experiencing domestic violence
and abuse.

Jewish Women's Aid

jwa.org.uk Helpline: 0808 801 0500

Legal, housing and benefits information, befriending and counselling for Jewish women.

Nour Domestic Violence Support

nour-dv.org.uk

Provides access to Islamic advisers, legal advisers, counselling and support.

Welsh Women's Aid

welshwomensaid.org.uk Helpline: 0808 80 10 800

Help for women and children facing domestic violence.

Scottish Women's Aid

scottishwomensaid.org.uk Helpline: 0800 027 1234

Help for women and children facing domestic violence.

Suzy Lamplugh Trust

suzylamplugh.org National stalking helpline: 0808 802 0300

Help and advice for victims of stalking.

Mind

mind.org.uk Helpline: 0300 123 3393

Mental health charity offering advice and support.

Beat

b-eat.co.uk Helpline: 0808 801 0677

Information and help on all aspects of eating disorders, including anorexia nervosa, bulimia nervosa, binge-eating disorder and related eating disorders.

Karma Nirvana

karmanirvana.org.uk Honour network helpline: 0800 5999 247
Supports all victims of honour-based abuse and forced marriage.

FORWARD

forwarduk.org.uk Helpline: 020 8960 4000
Advice, support and specialist healthcare for girls and women
affected by FGM.

Galop

galop.org.uk Helpline: 020 7704 2040
Advice and support for people who have experienced biphobia,
homophobia, transphobia, sexual violence or domestic abuse.
Also provides support for lesbian, gay, bi, trans and queer
people who have had problems with the police or have questions
about the criminal justice system.

NOTES

p. 10   **The term 'intersectionality'** ... scholarship.law.columbia. edu/books/255

p. 10   **'white supremacist, capitalist patriarchy'** ... mediaed. org/transcripts/Bell-Hooks-Transcript.pdf

p. 10   **The school dress codes** ... diversityis.com/activist s-and-researchers-say-school-dress-codes-unfairl y-target-african-american-girls

p. 10   **from colourful hijabs** ... theconversation.com/afro-hair-ho w-pupils-are-tackling-discriminatory-uniform-policies-159290

p. 10   **to black girls' hairstyles** ... bbc.co.uk/news/ newsbeat-45521094

p. 19   **The leading retailer** ... bbc.co.uk/news/business-40916607

p. 21   **suicide is the leading cause** ... england.nhs.uk/blog/tacklin g-the-root-causes-of-suicide

p. 22   **Take the boys' T-shirts** ... thesun.co.uk/living/4104363/thes e-are-the-most-sexist-kids-clothes-in-britain-and-they-were-all -for-sale-on-the-high-street

p. 22   **we're literally printing it** ... ibid.

p. 22   **Studies have repeatedly shown** ... theatlantic.com/science/ archive/2017/01/six-year-old-girls-already-have-gendered-belief s-about-intelligence/514340

p. 22   **This continues into adulthood** ... onlinelibrary.wiley.com/
doi/abs/10.1111/j.0021-9029.2006.00013.x

p. 24   **On average in the UK** ... bbc.co.uk/news/
education-34138287

p. 24   **Almost a third** ... endviolenceagainstwomen.org.uk/yougo
v-poll-exposes-high-levels-sexual-harassment-in-schools

p. 24   **Almost 80 per cent** ... theguardian.com/education/2021/
jun/10/sexual-harassment-is-a-routine-part-of-life-school
children-tell-ofsted

p. 24   **Ninety per cent** ... ibid.

p. 24   **Three-quarters of girls** ... ibid.

p. 24   **Ofsted inspectors carrying out** ... theguardian.com/
education/2021/jun/10/sexual-harassment-is-a-routine-par
t-of-life-schoolchildren-tell-ofsted

p. 26   **Female pupils from** ... liverpoolecho.co.uk/news/
liverpool-news/pupils-told-wear-shorts-under-20169922

p. 26   **'showing thigh'** ... globalnews.ca/news/3162741/more-tha
n-20-girls-sent-home-from-uk-school-because-uniform-sk
irts-were-too-short

p. 26   **'inappropriately' revealing** ... insider.com/teen-schoo
l-dress-code-yearbook-petition-2017-7

p. 26   **visible bra straps** ... insider.com/teens-protest-schools-br
a-strap-policy-2018-5

p. 26   **Shockingly, not one** ... upworthy.com/florida-high-schoo
l-yearbook-edits-breasts

p. 27   **while a nine-year-old** ... today.com/style/mississippi-schoo
l-punishes-9-year-old-girl-wearing-formfitting-clothes-t102483

p. 28   **dominated by white, male authors, composers** ...
theguardian.com/education/2020/sep/30/many-gcse-pupil
s-never-study-a-book-by-a-bame-author; stylist.co.uk/life/femal
e-authors-curriculum-gcse-a-level-woman-writers/195076;
theguardian.com/education/2015/aug/18/female-composers-
a-level-music-syllabus-petition

p. 28   **40 per cent of UK universities** ... inews.co.uk/news/
education/universities-failing-sexual-misconduct-victims-1072067

p. 28   **Research into Key Stage 3 texts** ... youtube.com/
watch?v=3Ca1q8tdGvc

p. 32   **When you are educated** ... independent.co.uk/news/uk/
politics/school-compulsory-lessons-colony-slave-trade-b1807571.
html

p. 34   **'I just prefer to exercise inside.'** runnersworld.com/uk/
training/a36278390/reclaim-the-run; nuffieldhealth.com/
article/almost-three-quarters-of-british-women-dont-feel-safe-
exercising-outdoors-in-the-dark

p. 34   **'I'm just not one of those people who can haggle for a
pay rise!'** peoplemanagement.co.uk/news/articles/most-wome
n-never-asked-pay-rise-survey-finds#gref

p. 34   **'I'm probably not well enough qualified for the job.'**
abcnews.go.com/Business/women-aggressive-men-applyin
g-jobs-hired-frequently-linkedin/story?id=61531741

p. 34   **'Perhaps I'm just not presenting my ideas in the right
way.'** mic.com/articles/189829/nearly-two-thirds-of-women-i
n-tech-say-their-ideas-are-ignored-until-a-man-repeats-them-s
tudy-shows

p. 34   **'I just can't seem to find enough hours in the
day.'** wbg.org.uk/wp-content/uploads/2020/04/
Accompanying-paper-FINAL.pdf

p. 34   **'I'm just not all that comfortable talking about what I
want in bed.'** nationalsexstudy.indiana.edu

p. 35   **A US study found that women** ... news.harvard.edu/
gazette/story/2020/02/men-better-than-women-at-self-promoti
on-on-job-leading-to-inequities

p. 35   **Just 12.5 per cent of women** ... weforum.org/
agenda/2018/04/women-are-still-not-asking-fo
r-pay-rises-here-s-why

p. 35   **Women are dramatically more likely** ... telegraph.
co.uk/business/2017/09/18/women-likely-men-underpaid-les
s-likely-complain

p. 36   **Data from hundreds of millions** ... abcnews.go.com/Business/
women-aggressive-men-applying-jobs-hired-frequently-linkedin/
story?id=61531741

p. 40   **estimated 54,000 women** ... theguardian.com/money/2015/
jul/24/maternity-leave-discrimination-54000-women-
lose-jobs-each-year-ehrc-report

p. 41 **when a heterosexual couple co-habit** . . . independent.
co.uk/life-style/women-men-household-chores-domest
ic-house-gender-norms-a9021586.html

p. 41 **During the COVID-19 lockdown** . . . peoplemanagement.
co.uk/news/articles/women-providing-two-thirds-more-ch
ildcare-than-men-during-lockdown#gref

p. 42 **That same LinkedIn study** . . . abcnews.
go.com/Business/women-aggressive-men-applyin
g-jobs-hired-frequently-linkedin/story?id=61531741

p. 42 **Research has repeatedly shown** . . . pnas.org/
content/109/41/16474

p. 42 **Studies have revealed similar** . . . hbswk.hbs.edu/item/
minorities-who-whiten-job-resumes-get-more-interviews

p. 42 **One in eight HR decision-makers** . . . peoplemanagement.
co.uk/news/articles/one-in-eight-employers-reluctant-to-
hire-women-who-might-have-children#gref; theguardian.
com/world/2018/sep/13/workplace-gender-discriminatio
n-remains-rife-survey-finds

p. 43 **In the span of a forty-year career** . . .
nwlc-ciw49tixgw5lbab.stackpathdns.com/wp-content/
uploads/2019/03/Women-and-the-Lifetime-Wage-Gap-v1.pdf

p. 43 **A TUC poll found** . . . tuc.org.uk/news/nearly-on
e-three-disabled-workers-surveyed-treated-unfai
rly-work-during-pandemic-new-tuc

p. 43 **Recent research from the Fawcett Society** . . .
fawcettsociety.org.uk/news/women-candidates-face-explicit-re
sistance-and-discrimination-within-political-parties

p. 43 **just 41 per cent of people** . . . bbc.com/worklife/articl
e/20210108-why-do-we-still-distrust-women-leaders

p. 44 **were educated at Oxbridge** . . . educationbusinessuk.
net/news/16122019/slight-fall-number-mps-wh
o-attended-university

p. 44 **went to private school** . . . gov.uk/government/news/
elitism-in-britain-2019

p. 45 **studies show that privileged, white men** . . . insight.
kellogg.northwestern.edu/article/hirable_like_me

p. 45   **Then throw in a recent investigation** . . . thetimes.co.uk/
article/new-tory-sleaze-row-as-donors-who-pay-3m-get-seat
s-in-house-of-lords-2575s6jmp

p. 45   **A woman's perceived deserved compensation** . . .
cultureplusconsulting.com/2018/03/10/gender-bias-wor
k-assertiveness-double-bind

p. 45   **Women are also dramatically more likely** . . .
psychologicalscience.org/news/minds-business/leading-whil
e-female-prepare-to-counter-the-backlash.html; gap.hks.
harvard.edu/social-incentives-gender-differences-propensity-ini
tiate-negotiations-sometimes-it-does-hurt-ask

p. 45   **And high-achieving women are** . . . fortune.
com/2014/08/26/performance-review-gender-bias

p. 46   **Like Ellen Pao** . . . businessinsider.com/reddit-doesnt-negotiat
e-salaries-ellen-pao-2015-6?r=US&IR=T

p. 46   **Reddit users signed petitions** . . . dailydot.com/unclick/elle
n-pao-reddit-ceo-petition-sexist

p. 46   **She was also referred to as** . . . vox.com/2015/7/8/8914661/
reddit-victoria-protest

p. 46   **It was significant** . . . dailydot.com/unclick/ellen-pao-reddi
t-ceo-petition-sexist; alphr.com/demographics-reddit; change.
org/p/ellen-k-pao-step-down-as-ceo-of-reddit-inc

p. 46   **At the time Pao left** . . . vox.com/2015/7/8/8914661/
reddit-victoria-protest

p. 47   **In 1920, MP Nancy Astor** . . . bbc.co.uk/news/
uk-politics-51612796

p. 47   **Tim Hunt spoke** . . . theguardian.com/uk-news/2015/jun/10/
nobel-scientist-tim-hunt-female-scientists-cause-trouble-for
-men-in-labs

p. 48   **One in eight American women** . . . adaa.org/find-help-for/
women/depression

p. 48   **Research in 2020 found** . . . theguardian.com/
society/2020/sep/14/uk-has-experienced-explosion-i
n-anxiety-since-2008-study-finds

p. 48   **research repeatedly showed a burgeoning crisis** . . . forbes.
com/sites/alicebroster/2020/09/25/coronavirus-has-caused-a-crisis-
in-womens-mental-health-according-to-study/?sh=38fd1ab673db

p. 52 **A study of over 2,300 women found ...** mic.com/
articles/113334/these-are-the-new-orgasm-statistics-eve
ry-woman-should-see

p. 52 **a $12 billion global pornography industry ...** bbc.co.uk/
news/technology-55333403

p. 55 **Peter Andre tweets ...** mirror.co.uk/3am/celebrity-news/
peter-andre-begs-katie-prices-24981105?utm_source=facebook
.com&utm_medium=social&utm_campaign=mirror_main&
fbclid=IwAR1tobcsDHQzxLKN2EXJyH9qEoyvyBjr58gkls9
M2izoepDFByaygufM34

p. 55 **200 million girls and women alive today ...** endfgm.eu/
female-genital-mutilation/what-is-fgm

p. 56 **She points to figures showing ...** rcog.org.uk/globalassets/
documents/news/britspag_labiaplastypositionstatement.pdf;
bbc.co.uk/news/health-40410459

p. 57 **When Nimco Ali ...** dailymail.co.uk/femail/article-2320665/
Female-Genital-Mutilation-cultural-violence-66-000-women
-UK-live-effects-FGM-victim-Nimko-Ali-hits-PC-societ
y-ignored-pain.html

p. 60 **'Sarah Everard: missing woman's case sends UK into
shock.'** aljazeera.com/news/2021/3/11/uk-in-shock-after-polic
e-officer-arrested-over-missing-woman

p. 60 **The day before Sarah disappeared ...** cheshire-live.co.uk/
news/chester-cheshire-news/familys-tribute-congleton-woma
n-found-19992894

p. 60 **The day after Sarah went missing ...** leicestermercury.
co.uk/news/leicester-news/man-accused-murdering-woma
n-found-5288994

p. 61 **On the same day ...** theoldhamtimes.co.uk/news/19145472.
family-pays-tribute-29-year-old-woman-found-dead-oldham;
manchestereveningnews.co.uk/news/greater-manchester-news/
woman-stabbed-multiple-times-kitchen-20202720

p. 61 **when her boyfriend was found guilty ...**
manchestereveningnews.co.uk/news/greater-manchester-news/
murdered-girlfriend-wrote-body-it-21156946

p. 61 **The day after that ...** walesonline.co.uk/news/wales-news/
school-describes-devastating-impact-death-20035530

p. 61 **Before the month was out** . . . kareningalasmith.com/tag/
counting-dead-women

p. 61 **Have you ever heard any of their names?** ibid.

p. 62 **98.6 per cent of perpetrators** . . . theguardian.com/
society/2020/jul/17/one-in-70-recorded-rapes-in-englan
d-and-wales-led-to-charge-last-year

p. 62 **women in Clapham told reporters** . . . mirror.co.uk/news/
uk-news/sarah-everard-missing-women-living-23631910

p. 69 **'jilted husband'** . . . dailymail.co.uk/news/article-9286147/
Jilted-husband-62-murdered-disabled-campaigner-wif
e-58-jailed-life.html

p. 69 **Or the deaths of 278 women** . . . theguardian.
com/society/2021/mar/07/end-femicide-278-dea
d-the-hidden-scandal-of-older-women-killed
-by-men?CMP=Share_iOSApp_Other

p. 69 **In a 2020 poll** . . . wearehourglass.org/sites/default/files/
inline-files/Safer%20Ageing%20Week_polling%20release%20
-%20Wales_V1.pdf

p. 71 **Metropolitan Police Commissioner Cressida
Dick gave a statement** . . . inews.co.uk/news/uk/sara
h-everard-cressida-dick-announcement-women-abduc
tion-human-remains-found-908525

p. 71 **the fact that over 70 per cent** . . . theguardian.com/
world/2021/mar/10/almost-all-young-women-in-the-uk-have-be
en-sexually-harassed-survey-finds

p. 72 **'Family tribute to woman found on fire in street'** . . . bbc.
com/news/uk-england-manchester-58104988.amp

p. 72 **'Devastated family of woman who died after being
found on fire "miss her every day"'** . . . mirror.co.uk/
news/uk-news/devastated-family-woman-who-died-24697052

p. 73 **Shadow Culture Secretary Jo Stevens** . . . hansard.
parliament.uk/Commons/2021-03-18/debates/6643456C-27C
1-4355-A8FF-ABDBDEB75288/TopicalQuestions#contributio
n-0FDD8079-A6DE-46CD-852F-6AB7946DE0A2

p. 74 **The MP in question, Ellie Reeves** . . . graziadaily.co.uk/
life/in-the-news/ellie-reeves-attorney-general-michael-ellis-rape
-conviction-rate

p. 74   **there is just a 1.4 per cent chance ...** theguardian.com/
society/2020/jul/17/one-in-70-recorded-rapes-in-englan
d-and-wales-led-to-charge-last-year

p. 75   **'find a safe alternative way to express their views' ...**
bbc.co.uk/news/uk-56379248

p. 75   **Police didn't seem particularly concerned ...**
mirror.co.uk/news/uk-news/breaking-sarah-everard-vigi
l-hundreds-23710104

p. 75   **linked to 2,000 cases of COVID-19 ...** bbc.co.uk/news/
uk-scotland-57667163

p. 75   **It was found that the police had 'acted
appropriately' ...** bbc.co.uk/news/uk-56574557

p. 76   **In dealing with such officers ...** theguardian.com/
uk-news/2021/jun/08/cressida-dick-admits-there-are-bad-uns-in
-the-metropolitan-police

p. 77   **Except that Wayne Couzens was reported ...** metro.
co.uk/2021/03/12/pc-wayne-couzens-flashed-woman-3-days-be
fore-sarah-everard-vanished-14231070

p. 77   **Dating as far back as 2015 ...** news.sky.com/story/sara
h-everard-calls-for-investigation-into-how-wayne-couzens-
stayed-a-police-officer-after-indecent-exposure-incidents-
12352734

p. 78   **By July that year ...** news.sky.com/story/twelv
e-officers-investigated-by-police-watchdog-over-case-of
-sarah-everards-killer-12352335

p. 78   **One of the officers being investigated ...** ibid.

p. 78   **Who allegedly shared 'jokes' on WhatsApp ...** thetimes.
co.uk/article/met-policeman-to-keep-job-after-sharing-murde
r-meme-during-everard-search-tz8vwqfl2

p. 78   **The same force, in fact ...** bbc.co.uk/news/
uk-england-london-57260505; independent.co.uk/news/uk/
crime/deniz-jaffer-jamie-lewis-guilty-jailed-whatsapp-b1970726.
html

p. 79   **sharing misogynistic, racist and homophobic
messages ...** independent.co.uk/news/uk/crime/wayn
e-couzens-whatsapp-met-police-b1930946.html

p. 79 **nicknamed him 'The Rapist'** ... inews.co.uk/news/uk/
wayne-couzens-the-rapist-nickname-why-known-as-sarah-ev
erard-killer-explained-1227129

p. 79 **The woman told the BBC** ... bbc.co.uk/news/
uk-england-london-56409023

p. 80 **The force told the BBC** ... bbc.co.uk/news/
uk-england-55848743

p. 80 **of almost 11,000 cases of 'exposure and voyeurism'** ...
theguardian.com/uk-news/2021/oct/01/police-log-1000
0-indecent-exposure-cases-but-fewer-than-600-reach-court

p. 82 **Almost 600 sexual misconduct allegations** ...
theguardian.com/uk-news/2021/mar/20/revealed-the-grim-lis
t-of-sex-abuse-claims-against-metropolitan-police

p. 82 **a West Mercia Police officer is on bail** ... bbc.co.uk/news/
uk-england-hereford-worcester-56596141

p. 82 **a probationary officer at West Midlands Police** ... bbc.
co.uk/news/uk-england-coventry-warwickshire-56459217

p. 82 **an officer from West Yorkshire Police** ... itv.com/news/
calendar/2021-04-21/sergeant-ben-lister-west-yorkshire-police
-officer-denies-rape-and-sexual-assault

p. 82 **the Met is currently investigating allegations** ... bbc.
co.uk/news/uk-56581835

p. 83 **It had taken almost two decades** ... chroniclelive.
co.uk/news/north-east-news/predatory-police-officer-se
x-vulnerable-21361148

p. 83 **In 2021, six officers** ... theguardian.com/
uk-news/2021/jan/08/hampshire-police-officers-sacke
d-over-shameful-language

p. 83 **They had inadvertently recorded themselves** ...
telegraph.co.uk/women/womens-life/11957145/Domesti
c-violence-British-police-voicemail-called-victim-a-slag.html

p. 84 **In 2022, the IOPC released** ... https://www.policeconduct.
gov.uk/sites/default/files/Operation%20Hotton%20
Learning%20report%20-%20January%202022.pdf

p. 84 **Yet in spite of the overwhelming evidence** ... https://
www.theguardian.com/uk-news/2022/feb/01/met-officers-joke
d-raping-women-police-watchdog-racist

p. 84 **Most damning of all ...** https://www.bbc.co.uk/news/uk-england-london-60215575

p. 85 **Data gathered by the Centre for Women's Justice ...** centreforwomensjustice.org.uk/news/2020/3/9/police-officers-allowed-to-abuse-with-impunity-in-the-locker-room-culture-of-uk-forces-super-complaint-reveals

p. 85 **'I'm a police officer, no one's going to believe you.'** assets.publishing.service.gov.uk/government/uploads/system/uploads/attachment_data/file/913084/Police_perpetrated_domestic_abuse.pdf

p. 85 **A 2016 survey ...** unison.org.uk/content/uploads/2018/08/UNISON-LSE-report-Time-to-stamp-out-sexual-harassment-in-the-police-1.pdf

p. 86 **the fact that three in four domestic abuse cases ...** theguardian.com/society/2021/jun/23/domestic-abuse-cases-end-without-charge-england-wales

p. 86 **Even after a victim has finally ...** safelives.org.uk/policy-evidence/about-domestic-abuse/how-long-do-people-live-domestic-abuse-and-when-do-they-get

p. 86 **domestic abuse survivors report to police 2.8 times ...** ibid.

p. 86 **Instead, evidence reveals a postcode lottery ...** theguardian.com/society/2021/jun/23/domestic-abuse-cases-end-without-charge-england-wales

p. 87 **Someone who didn't feel safe ...** theguardian.com/uk-news/2021/oct/01/police-must-win-back-public-confidence-after-sarah-everard-case-says-minister

p. 88 **'It just makes you more of a harder target' ...** bbc.co.uk/news/newsbeat-59235121

p. 89 **Women like Valerie Forde ...** sistahspace.org/valerieslaw

p. 89 **Or the sex worker who was assaulted ...** inews.co.uk/opinion/how-sex-workers-who-are-sexually-assaulted-are-being-failed-by-the-justice-system-328027

p. 90 **15 per cent of those who experience sexual violence ...** rapecrisis.org.uk/get-informed/about-sexual-violence/statistics-sexual-violence

p. 90 **An investigation found that a fifth ...** justiceinspectorates.

gov.uk/hmicfrs/wp-content/uploads/crime-recording-makin
g-the-victim-count.pdf

p. 91   **We saw it in Rotherham** . . . theguardian.com/uk-news/2017/
apr/01/sammy-woodhouse-interview

p. 92   **Men still make up at least two-thirds** . . . theguardian.
com/uk-news/2021/mar/16/institutional-misogyny-erode
s-womens-trust-in-uk-police

p. 93   **These twenty-seven referrals** . . . theguardian.com/
society/2021/oct/10/a-third-of-police-forces-referred-sex-a
ssault-claims-to-watchdog-sarah-everard

p. 93   **we know from freedom-of-information requests** . . .
independent.co.uk/news/uk/crime/sexual-assault-harassmen
t-metropolitan-police-metoo-london-a8845811.html

p. 94   **Police Commissioner Philip Allott, who was
interviewed** . . . bbc.co.uk/news/uk-england-york-nort
h-yorkshire-58762029

p. 95   **Since 2016–17, rape prosecutions have plummeted** . . .
theguardian.com/law/2021/jul/22/cps-accused-of-betrayin
g-victims-as-prosecutions-hit-record-low; statista.com/
statistics/283100/recorded-rape-offences-in-england-and-wales

p. 95   **The report included** . . . endviolenceagainstwomen.org.uk/
our-judicial-review-evidence-against-cps-handed-over-to-govern
ment-2

p. 96   **noted a whistle-blower** . . . endviolenceagainstwomen.org.
uk/wp-content/uploads/XX-Statement.pdf

p. 97   **extensive evidence put forward by the EVAW** . . .
endviolenceagainstwomen.org.uk/wp-content/uploads/
JOINT-MEDIA-BRIEFING-15.3.21.pdf

p. 97   **Even though it coincided** . . . ibid.

p. 97   **data from the CPS itself showed** . . . ibid.

p. 97   **The same judiciary** . . . assets.publishing.service.gov.uk/
government/uploads/system/uploads/attachment_data/
file/918529/diversity-of-the-judiciary-2020-statistics-web.pdf

p. 97   **And, in the Supreme Court** . . . supremecourt.uk/about/
biographies-of-the-justices.html

p. 98 **Less consideration seems to have been given ...**
manchestereveningnews.co.uk/news/greater-manchester-news/
oldham-councillor-urges-review-after-20183218

p. 99 **Ultimately, he was convicted ...** theguardian.com/
uk-news/2021/feb/18/anthony-williams-killed-wife-act-of-g
reat-violence-jailed-for-five-years

p. 99 **So surreal, so ridiculous ...** theguardian.com/
uk-news/2021/feb/18/anthony-williams-killed-wife-act-of-g
reat-violence-jailed-for-five-years

p. 99 **a four-year study by the Centre for Women's Justice ...**
centreforwomensjustice.org.uk/women-who-kill

p. 100 **The judge and prosecution described ...** independent.
co.uk/news/uk/crime/judge-calls-victim-13-sexual-pr
edator-outcry-41-year-old-man-walks-free-after-adm
itting-sex-girl-8748494.html

p. 100 **In 2017, an Idaho judge ...** theguardian.com/us-news/2017/
feb/08/idaho-judge-rape-social-media-twin-falls

p. 100 **In a 2018 rape trial ...** bbc.co.uk/news/
world-europe-46207304

p. 101 **When a top court prosecutor ...** worcesternews.
co.uk/news/14776023.jailed-top-court-prosecutor-fro
m-worcester-jailed-for-six-years-after-trying-to-kill-his-wife
-in-frenzied-knife-attack

p. 101 **Daniel Lancaster, who claimed ...** lancashiretelegraph.
co.uk/news/9185784.family-colne-strangling-victi
m-disappointed-verdict

p. 101 **James Morton, twenty-four ...** bbc.co.uk/news/uk-englan
d-nottinghamshire-40670225

p. 101 **Between 2009 and 2019 ...** theguardian.com/society/2019/
jul/25/fatal-hateful-rise-of-choking-during-sex

p. 101 **When millionaire John Broadhurst ...** birminghammail.
co.uk/black-country/natalie-connolly-killer-joh
n-broadhurst-19023076

p. 103 **In the wake of a highly controversial ...** theguardian.
com/news/2018/dec/04/rugby-rape-trial-ireland-belfast-case

p. 105 **Chris Henley QC had written ...** criminalbar.com/
resources/news/cba-monday-message-11-02-19

p. 105 **'I'm not aware of any evidence . . .'** telegraph.co.uk/
news/2019/04/03/sexism-uk-courts-exaggerated-lord-chief-ju
stice-suggests-cases

p. 105 **A 2020 study of over 700 solicitors . . .** legalcheek.
com/2020/02/over-half-of-female-lawyers-have-experienc
ed-or-witnessed-sexism-at-work

p. 105 **In the same year . . .** bbc.co.uk/news/
uk-england-essex-54281111

p. 106 **And a senior government barrister . . .** dailymail.co.uk/
news/article-9030023/Lawyer-55-took-upskirt-pictures-AVO
IDS-struck-blaming-Brexit-planning-stress.html

p. 107 **Out of 554 students surveyed . . .** theguardian.com/society/
2021/oct/29/research-reveals-rapes-and-assaults-admitted-
to-by-male-uk-students?CMP=Share_iOSApp_Other&fbclid
=IwAR2oseM3iTowIeZKuAk1DqCZayZHxrtlQujVu6Hw
Q80Q-sgMJK-HqlDdSpQ

p. 109 **A whopping three-quarters say . . .** tuc.org.uk/sites/
default/files/SexualHarassmentreport2016.pdf

p. 109 **only fourteen tribunal claims . . .** publications.parliament.
uk/pa/cm201719/cmselect/cmwomeq/725/72507.htm

p. 113 **There is no small irony . . .** members.parliament.uk/parties/
lords/by-gender; lordslibrary.parliament.uk/research-briefings/
lln-2019-0150

p. 113 **There are currently just sixty-five.** commonslibrary.
parliament.uk/research-briefings/sn01156

p. 113 **Women comprise only a third . . .** gov.uk/government/
ministers

p. 114 **It is this overwhelmingly white . . .** womensaid.org.
uk/womens-aid-responds-to-the-governments-funding-ann
ouncement

p. 114 **It 'consistently failed' . . .** theguardian.com/world/2021/
may/08/uk-government-failed-to-consider-gender-in-its-respon
se-to-covid-pandemic

p. 114 **working mothers losing their jobs . . .** theguardian.com/
world/2020/may/27/working-mothers-interrupted-more-ofte
n-than-fathers-in-lockdown-study

p. 114 **new mothers traumatically forced** ... inews.co.uk/news/
childbirth-campaign-pregnant-women-give-birth-alone-coronavi
rus-rules-change-635774

p. 114 **pregnant women left unprotected** ... theguardian.
com/world/2021/apr/21/pregnant-women-need-better-covi
d-safety-at-work-say-campaigners

p. 114 **research by the Women's Budget Group** ... wbg.org.uk/
media/press-releases/investment-in-scandinavian-style-univers
al-care-would-create-more-than-2-million-jobs

p. 114 **women, who are at greater risk** ... theguardian.com/
world/2021/may/04/women-jobs-risk-covid-pandemi
c-uk-analysis

p. 115 **In that nearly three-week period** ... bbc.co.uk/news/
uk-53781734

p. 115 **Enter hereditary (unelected) peer** ... theguardian.com/
commentisfree/2021/nov/10/we-need-to-protect-breastfeedin
g-women-from-voyeurs-so-why-did-the-debate-get-so-weird

p. 116 **Nimco Ali has described** ... independent.co.uk/news/
uk/home-news/jeremy-hunt-fgm-survivor-nimco-ali-google-o
rgasm-female-genital-mutilation-health-secretary-a7652521.html

p. 116 **This means that many women** ... edition.cnn.
com/2021/09/09/politics/abbott-abortion-fact-check/index.
html

p. 116 **When asked about the impact** ... independent.
co.uk/news/world/americas/us-politics/
texas-abortion-law-rape-abbott-b1915879.html

p. 117 **As an MP, you're expected** ... inews.co.uk/news/politics/
stella-creasy-pregnant-mp-sue-parliament-like-for-like-m
aternity-leave-rejected-1076752

p. 117 **This leaves women like** ... theguardian.com/
lifeandstyle/2019/feb/12/tulip-siddiq-i-needed-a-caesarean-i
nstead-i-was-at-parliament

p. 118 **One MP told the BBC** ... bbc.co.uk/news/
uk-wales-politics-52785157

p. 118 **Labour MP Diane Abbott, who** ... theguardian.
com/politics/2017/sep/05/diane-abbott-more-abused-tha
n-any-other-mps-during-election

p. 118 **A UK poll found** ... independent.co.uk/news/uk/politics/
westminster-sexual-harassment-one-five-report-leaked-mps
-lords-staff-a8199401.html

p. 118 **In 2019, after a slew of allegations** ... theguardian.com/
commentisfree/2019/jul/01/mp-expenses-violence-misogyn
y-harassment-recall-commons

p. 118 **An inquiry found** ... theguardian.com/politics/2020/aug/03/
did-westminsters-culture-of-impunity-ever-go-away

p. 119 **It's hard to believe** ... theguardian.com/politics/2021/
nov/01/conservative-party-readmits-mp-sexually-harassed-staff-
rob-roberts

p. 119 **Meanwhile, when both a** ... theguardian.com/
politics/2021/nov/21/sex-life-scoured-by-media-after-stanl
ey-johnson-allegations-mp-claims

p. 119 **a fellow MP openly told the press** ... bbc.co.uk/news/
uk-politics-59451874

p. 119 **In 2021, Home Secretary** ... theguardian.com/
lifeandstyle/2021/oct/09/new-888-service-to-protect-wome
n-wins-patels-support

p. 121 **He who had mocked** ... bbc.co.uk/news/
uk-politics-45083275

p. 121 **He who wrote** ... scotsman.com/read-this/boris-johnson-ha
s-refused-to-apologise-for-past-sexist-comments-despite-his-ple
dge-to-address-the-issue-of-casual-sexism-3170177

p. 121 **They reveal a man who** ... mirror.co.uk/news/uk-news/
voting-tory-cause-your-wife-8274342

p. 121 **Johnson was accused by a journalist** ... dailymail.
co.uk/debate/article-10209893/Sins-father-sound-familiar-A
NDREW-PIERCE-examines-claims-against-Stanley-Johnson.
html

p. 122 **The disclosures were 'shocking and abhorrent'** ... bbc.
co.uk/news/uk-56566442

p. 123 **Its own Women and Equalities Select Committee** ...
publications.parliament.uk/pa/cm201617/cmselect/
cmwomeq/91/9105.htm#_idTextAnchor009

p. 123 **It was that the problem** ... endviolenceagainstwomen.org.
uk/campaign/metoo-at-school

p. 123 **The media ran articles ...** standard.co.uk/insider/everyone-
s-invited-teenage-boys-suffering-soma-sara-b942057.html

p. 127 **This portrayal, which ...** theguardian.com/society/2015/
dec/29/charlotte-proudman-feminazi-barrister-linkedin-sexis
m-row; metro.co.uk/2021/07/07/piers-morgan-slams-naom
i-osaka-again-after-netflix-doc-announcement-14889487

p. 127 **In the year following the resurgence ...** momentive.ai/en/
newsroom/men-continue-to-pull-back-in-wake-of-metoo

p. 128 **One study found ...** brunel.ac.uk/news-and-events/
news/articles/Newspapers-key-to-spreadin
g-MeToo-message-in-Britain

p. 128 **when Scottish First Minister ...** theguardian.com/
politics/2015/apr/21/tories-and-rightwing-press-resort-
to-sexist-sturgeon-jibes

p. 128 **when articles are published ridiculing ...** spectator.
co.uk/article/the-row-over-racist-abuse-of-diane-abbott-sho
ws-how-far-momentum-will-sink

p. 131 **The most recent data, from 2017 ...** womeninjournalism.
co.uk/the-tycoon-and-the-escort-the-business-of-portraying
-women-in-newspapers

p. 131 **A UNESCO survey in 2020 ...** en.unesco.org/news/unesco
s-global-survey-online-violence-against-women-journalists

p. 131 **A UK-specific study ...** digiday.com/media/sobering-finding
s-one-five-young-women-media-advertising-sexually-harassed

p. 131 **The Second Source ...** independent.co.uk/voices/sexua
l-harassment-journalism-take-stand-abuse-assault-sexis
m-a8035336.html

p. 132 **A Women in Journalism report found ...**
womeninjournalism.co.uk/wp-content/uploads/2018/02/Seen_
but_not_heard1.pdf

p. 132 **A 2018 study revealed ...** tandfonline.com/doi/full/10.1080/
14680777.2018.1468797

p. 132 **A significant number of high-profile female MPs ...** bbc.
co.uk/news/election-2019-50246969

p. 132 **Or that they might become the subject ...** theguardian.
com/lifeandstyle/the-womens-blog-with-jane-martinson/2011/
apr/27/telegraph-website-whose-boobs-are-these

p. 133   **'I'm being boycotted by Hollywood.'** thetimes.co.uk/article/
johnny-depp-interview-im-being-boycotted-by-hollywood-zpllqzl5k

p. 133   **The newspaper articles read . . .** dailymail.co.uk/tvshowbiz/
article-10017929/Johnny-Depp-claims-hes-victim-cancel-c
ulture-amid-50m-defamation-lawsuit.html

p. 133   **But remember what we know . . .** losangeles.cbslocal.
com/2017/11/17/cant-touch-this-sexual-assault-claims-destr
oy-the-careers-of-powerful-men-but-not-the-president

p. 133   **Then there's the Audi advert . . .** independent.co.uk/news/
business/news/audi-advert-china-sexist-watch-video-women-us
ed-cars-perfect-wife-a7849016.html

p. 133   **the ad that showed women home-schooling . . .**
theguardian.com/uk-news/2021/jan/28/no-10-pulls-sexist-covi
d-ad-showing-all-chores-done-by-women

p. 135   **a family of children jumped out . . .** dailymail.co.uk/news/
article-9965793/Family-flee-pyjamas-lorry-deliberately-dri
ven-home-domestic-row.html

p. 135   **A man named Jake Davison . . .** reuters.com/world/uk/
british-shooter-named-jake-davison-2021-08-13

p. 136   **When the BBC mistook . . .** buzzfeed.com/adeonibada/evenin
g-standard-apologised-bell-ribeiro-addy

p. 136   **Meanwhile, Diane Abbott . . .** theguardian.com/
commentisfree/2017/feb/14/racism-misogyny-politics-onlin
e-abuse-minorities?CMP=soc_3156

p. 137   **In 2021, one female police officer . . .** theguardian.
com/uk-news/2021/mar/16/institutional-misogyny-erode
s-womens-trust-in-uk-police

p. 137   **A report from the Home Affairs Committee . . .**
committees.parliament.uk/committee/83/
home-affairs-committee/news/157006/urgent-actio
n-needed-to-tackle-deep-rooted-and-persistent-
racial-disparities-in-policing

p. 137   **Another 2021 report found . . .** bbc.co.uk/news/
uk-england-manchester-57982273

p. 137   **meanwhile, government figures showed . . .**
ethnicity-facts-figures.service.gov.uk/crime-justice-and-the-law/
policing/stop-and-search/latest

p. 137   **in 2018, UN human rights experts . . .** ohchr.
org/EN/NewsEvents/Pages/DisplayNews.
aspx?NewsID=22997&LangID=E

p. 139   **There are the black women . . .** theguardian.com/
global-development/2021/jan/15/black-women-in-the-uk-fou
r-times-more-likely-to-die-in-pregnancy-or-childbirth

p. 139   **There are the disabled women . . .** wbg.org.uk/analysis/201
8-wbg-briefing-disabled-women-and-austerity/#:~:text=14%20
million%20people%20in%20the,have%20someone%20with%20
a%20disability

p. 139   **And there are the migrant women . . .** bbc.co.uk/news/
uk-46371441

p. 141   **The often-quoted ONS statistics . . .** rapecrisis.org.uk/med
ia/2396/c-decriminalisation-of-rape-report-cwj-evaw-imkaan
-rcew-nov-2020.pdf

p. 141   **There was little discussion of . . .** sisofrida.org/the-impact-o
f-covid-19-on-disabled-women-from-sisters-of-frida

p. 141   **Nor was much said about . . .** bbc.co.uk/news/av/uk-55133088

p. 141   **This might take the form of . . .** metro.co.uk/2019/10/12/
police-seize-disabled-activists-wheelchairs-ahead-extinction
-rebellion-protests-10896624

p. 142   **Or a justice system . . .** endviolenceagainstwomen.org.uk/
wp-content/uploads/FINAL-living-in-a-hostile-environment-fo
r-Web-and-sharing-.pdf

p. 142   **Or a CPS . . .** mdx.ac.uk/news/2021/01/
bame-criminal-justice-system

p. 142   **A society in which black . . .** endviolenceagainstwomen.
org.uk/wp-content/uploads/Joint-Briefing-for-Meg-Hillie
r-MP-Debate-EVAW-Imkaan.pdf

p. 142   **A government led by . . .** businessinsider.com/boris-johnso
n-record-sexist-homophobic-and-racist-comments-bumboys-
piccaninnies-2019-6?r=US&IR=T

p. 143   **Reporting on the Atlanta incident . . .** nytimes.com/
live/2021/03/17/us/shooting-atlanta-acworth

p. 145   **In the wake of her death . . .** itv.com/news/2021-09-22/
sabina-nessa-more-than-200-alarms-handed-to-women-after-tea
chers-death

p. 145 **The male leader of her city's council** ... bbc.co.uk/news/
uk-england-devon-59490899

p. 147 **When a media mob hounds** ... marieclaire.co.uk/news/
celebrity-news/emma-watson-paparazzi-took-pictures-up-my-ski
rt-on-my-18th-birthday-14485

p. 149 **It extends from senior Australian firefighters** ...
theage.com.au/national/victoria/stripper-club-culture-senio
r-firefighter-calls-out-the-sexual-harassment-she-s-end
ured-20210905-p580w3.html

p. 149 **in Germany, where a model in a cycle helmet** ...
theguardian.com/media/2019/mar/24/german-bike-safety-a
d-featuring-model-in-bra-and-helmet-sexist

p. 149 **A survey of women journalists** ... niemanlab.org/2021/07/
one-of-the-main-reasons-why-women-leave-half-of-women-jour
nalists-in-africa-surveyed-have-been-sexually-harassed-at-work

p. 149 **In 2021, a judge in Switzerland** ... swissinfo.ch/
eng/swiss-protest-against-court-ruling-reducing-rapist-s
-sentence/46852284

p. 149 **A judge in India** ... aljazeera.com/news/2021/3/3/thousand
s-in-india-demand-top-judge-resign-over-rape-remarks

p. 149 **A judge in Peru** ... dailymail.co.uk/news/article-8914001/
Peru-judges-rule-rape-case-womans-red-underwear-signalled
-willing-sex.html

p. 150 **there are estimated to be** ... huffingtonpost.co.uk/entry/
the-rape-kit-backlog-shows-exactly-how-we-regard-women-in-
this-country_n_5acfb5e1e4b016a07e9a8c65

p. 150 **research suggests that up to 40 per cent** ...
womenandpolicing.org/violenceFS.asp

p. 150 **and fewer than 1 per cent** ... washingtonpost.com/
business/2018/10/06/less-than-percent-rapes-lead-felony-convict
ions-least-percent-victims-face-emotional-physical-consequences

p. 150 **This is also a country in which Indigenous** ... dss.gov.au/
sites/default/files/documents/08_2014/national_plan1.pdf

p. 150 **Indeed, it has been pointed out** ... theguardian.com/
society/2021/sep/06/indigenous-australians-need-own-plan-to
-reduce-violence-against-women-summit-told

p. 152 **He was ordered to pay** ... manchestereveningnews.co.uk/
news/greater-manchester-news/businessman-branded-ex-wif
e-bacon-16475342

p. 152 **In Texas, the new** ... aninjusticemag.com/does-the-bodil
y-autonomy-of-the-dead-matter-more-than-women-6e41ce0cb41c

p. 157 **There is the forensic, meticulous report** ... rapecrisis.
org.uk/media/2396/c-decriminalisation-of-rape-r
eport-cwj-evaw-imkaan-rcew-nov-2020.pdf

p. 157 **There are the solutions** ... static1.squarespace.com/static/
5f7d9f4addc689717e6ea200/t/607eea86aaa24a6d365cf3ba/16189
30331127/2018+%7C+Summary+of+the+Alternative+Bill.pdf

p. 158 **We also have the Women's Budget Group's** ... wbg.org.
uk/wp-content/uploads/2020/10/WBG-Report-v10.pdf

p. 158 **But the decisions about how** ... ft.com/content/c2f9639
d-455c-4e2b-9d75-81385f875150

p. 159 **The annual social and economic cost** ... gov.uk/government/
publications/the-economic-and-social-costs-of-domestic-abuse

p. 159 **Investment in early childhood education and care** ...
thesector.com.au/2019/06/20/pwc-report-shows-for-ever
y-dollar-invested-in-ecec-two-are-returned/

p. 159 **Companies with a more diverse workforce** ...
mckinsey.com/business-functions/organization/our-insights/
why-diversity-matters

p. 159 **Empowering women and** ... unwomen.org/en/what-we-do/
economic-empowerment/facts-and-figures

p. 160 **And even that unambitious target** ... theguardian.
com/society/2021/oct/21/government-will-take-years-hi
t-rape-charges-target-data

p. 161 **Sure, we can make it illegal** ... assets.publishing.service.
gov.uk/government/uploads/system/uploads/attachment_data/
file/509500/BIS-16-145-pregnancy-and-maternity-related-dis
crimination-and-disadvantage-summary.pdf

p. 161 **A 2018 YouGov poll showed** ... yougov.co.uk/
topics/resources/articles-reports/2018/12/01/
publics-attitudes-sexual-consent

p. 161 **And research has attributed 13.5 per cent** ... stylist.
co.uk/health/women/fearless-future-campaign/520763